JUNE 03

Test Results for Disk Imaging Tools: EnCase 3.20

NCJ 200031

Sarah V. Hart
Director

This report was prepared for the National Institute of Justice, U.S. Department of Justice, by the Office of Law Enforcement Standards of the National Institute of Standards and Technology under Interagency Agreement 94–IJ–R–004.

The National Institute of Justice is a component of the Office of Justice Programs, which also includes the Bureau of Justice Assistance, the Bureau of Justice Statistics, the Office of Juvenile Justice and Delinquency Prevention, and the Office for Victims of Crime.

Contents

Introduction

The Computer Forensics Tool Testing (CFTT) project is the joint effort of the National Institute of Justice, the National Institute of Standards and Technology (NIST), the U. S. Department of Defense, the Technical Support Working Group, and other related agencies. The objective of the CFTT project is to provide measurable assurance to practitioners, researchers, and other applicable users that the tools used in computer forensics investigations provide accurate results. Accomplishing this requires the development of specifications and test methods for computer forensics tools and subsequent testing of specific tools against those specifications.

The test results provide the information necessary for developers to improve tools, users to make informed choices, and the legal community and others to understand the tools' capabilities. The use of well-recognized methodologies for conformance and quality testing serves as the foundation of our approach for testing computer forensics tools. Plus, in an effort to further develop the specifications and test methods, we encourage the entire forensics community to visit the CFTT Web site (*http://www.cftt.nist.gov*), where drafts are accessible for both commentary and review.

This document reports the results from testing EnCase 3.20, a commonly used disk imaging tool, against *Disk Imaging Tool Specification, Version 3.1.6,* developed by CFTT staff and available at *http://www.cftt.nist.gov/DI-spec-3-1-6.doc*. This specification identifies the top-level disk imaging tool requirements as—

- The tool shall make a bit-stream duplicate or an image of an original disk or partition.
- The tool shall not alter the original disk.
- The tool shall log I/O errors.
- The tool's documentation shall be correct.

Note: The test methodology is for software tools that copy or image hard disk drives. It does not cover analog media or digital media such as cell phones or personal digital assistants (PDAs).

Test Results for Disk Imaging Tools: EnCase 3.20

Tool Tested:	EnCase 3.20
Operating Systems:	Windows 2000 (5.00.2195), Windows 98, and Windows 98 DOS (Version 4.10.2222)
Supplier:	Guidance Software
Address:	572 East Green Street, Suite 300
	Pasadena, CA 91101
Phone:	626–229–9191
Web:	*http://www.guidancesoftware.com*

1.   Results Summary by Requirements

The tool shall make a bit-stream duplicate or an image of an original disk or partition.
EnCase, with one exception, correctly and completely copied all disk sectors to an image file in the test cases that were run. EnCase, with two other exceptions, correctly and completely restored all disk sectors to a destination drive in the test cases that were run. The three exceptions are the following:

1. If the basic input/output system (BIOS) interface is chosen to access integrated drive electronics (IDE) hard drives on an older computer using a legacy BIOS that underreports the number of cylinders on the drive, then there may be a small area of sectors at the end of the drive that is not accessed. The sectors in this area are usually not used by commercial software. If direct access using the advance technology attachment (ATA) interface is chosen instead, EnCase accesses every sector of the hard drive.
2. For certain partition types (FAT32 and NTFS), a logical restore of a partition is not an exact duplicate of the original. The vendor documentation states that a logical restore cannot be verified as an exact copy of the source and is not recommended when seeking to create a bit-stream duplicate of the source. For FAT32 partitions, two file system control values (not part of any data file) are adjusted during restoration of an image to a destination. This adjustment is confined to about 8 bytes of sector 1 and the first sector of the FAT table (and FAT table backup copy) of the partition. For NTFS partitions, other changes were made to about 35 sectors of the partition. In no case was there any effect on sectors used in data files. All sectors of the image file accurately reflect the original sectors. These changes to a restored partition (logical volume) may be a consequence of the Windows shutdown process.
3. In the Windows 2000 environment, a hard drive may appear to have fewer sectors than are actually available on the drive. This has two consequences. First, an attempt to restore an entire drive to a drive of an identical size from Windows 2000 does not restore all sectors imaged from the source to the destination. Second, if restoring to a drive larger than the source and the *wipe excess sectors* option is selected, then not all the excess sectors are wiped. Restoring in a Windows 98 environment did not exhibit this anomaly.

The tool shall not alter the original disk.
For all the test cases that were run, EnCase never altered the original hard drive.

The tool shall be able to verify the integrity of a disk image file.
For all of the test cases that were run, EnCase always identified image files that had been modified.

The tool shall log I/O errors.
For all of the test cases that were run, EnCase always logged I/O errors.

The tool's documentation shall be correct.
The tool documentation available was the *EnCase Reference Manual, Version 3.0, Revision 3.18*. In some cases, the software behavior was not documented or was ambiguous.

2.   Anomalies

This section describes three anomalies found during the testing of EnCase 3.20 against the disk imaging requirements in *Disk Imaging Tool Specification, Version 3.1.6*. The behavior observed in these anomalies should not be interpreted as necessarily representing unacceptable behavior for an imaging tool. Some of the anomalies may only need more detailed documentation by the tool vendor. However, the tool user must be aware of these behaviors since they may affect the quality and completeness of a forensic investigation.

The following anomalies were found:

1.   **BIOS anomaly.** For IDE hard drives on computers with a legacy BIOS, if the legacy BIOS underreports the number of cylinders on the drive and the BIOS is used to access the drive, then there may be a small area of sectors at the end of the drive that is not accessed. The sectors in this area are usually not used by commercial software.
2.   **Logical restore anomaly.** For certain partition types (FAT32 and NTFS), a logical restore of a partition is not an exact duplicate of the original. The vendor documentation states that a logical restore cannot be verified as an exact copy of the source and is not recommended when seeking to create a bit-stream duplicate of the source. For FAT32 partitions, two file system control values (not part of any data file) are adjusted as a side effect of restoring an image to a destination. This adjustment is confined to about 8 bytes of sector 1 and the first sector of the FAT table (and FAT table backup copy) of the partition. For NTFS partitions, other changes were made to about 35 sectors of the partition. In no case was there any effect on sectors used in data files. All sectors of the image file accurately reflected the original sectors. These changes to a restored partition (logical volume) may be a consequence of the Windows shutdown process.
3.   **Restore size anomaly.** In the Windows 2000 environment, a hard drive may appear to have fewer sectors than are actually available on the drive. This has two consequences. First, an attempt to restore an entire drive to a drive of an identical size from Windows 2000 does not restore all sectors imaged from the source to the destination. Second, if restoring to a drive larger than the source and the *wipe excess sectors* option is selected, then not all the excess sectors are wiped. Restoring in a Windows 98 environment did not exhibit this anomaly. This is documented on the EnCase Web site but not in the manual (Version 3.0, Revision 3.18) distributed with EnCase 3.20.

The scope of each anomaly is indicated in Table 2-1. An anomaly can manifest in either an image file, a restored copy, or both. A restored copy means a copy of the original drive produced by the EnCase restore operation.

Table 2-1. Scope of Anomalies

Anomaly	Scope
BIOS	Image and restored copy.
Logical restore	Restored copy. By examining the image file, it was verified that the anomaly is only in the restored copy.
Restore size	Restored copy only.

2.1 Sectors Missed in Legacy BIOS Access

A legacy BIOS is defined to be a BIOS that does not implement the extensions to interrupt 13h BIOS services described in the standard *ANSI INCITS 347-2001 BIOS Enhanced Disk Drive Services*. This standard was developed by T13, a Technical Committee for the InterNational Committee on Information Technology Standards (INCITS), under *Project 1386D, BIOS Enhanced Disk Drive Services*. INCITS is accredited by and operates under rules approved by the American National Standards Institute (ANSI). Further information is available at *http://www.t13.org*.

An extended BIOS (referred to as XBIOS) is defined as a BIOS that implements the extensions to interrupt 13h BIOS services described in *Project 1386D, BIOS Enhanced Disk Drive Services*.

EnCase does not access (i.e., read or write) all usable sectors on a hard drive if the legacy BIOS underreports the size of the hard drive and EnCase uses BIOS access rather than direct access by the ATA interface. If this anomaly occurs while EnCase 3.20 is reading a source drive, then the EnCase image file will be missing a small number of sectors from the end of the hard drive. If this anomaly occurs during *zero backfilling* of the destination drive, then the backfilling is not done for a small number of sectors at the end of the hard drive. When the anomaly occurs during the restore of an image, then part of the image at the end of the destination hard drive might not be restored. These sectors at the end of a hard drive are not normally used on a system with a legacy BIOS for any purpose by Microsoft operating systems or by typical application programs. These sectors are accessible from a Microsoft operating system by special tools and could be used by other operating systems such as Linux or FreeBSD UNIX.

A physical hard drive may have a different physical geometry from the logical geometry presented by the BIOS. This is because the legacy BIOS interface can only present a hard drive with less than 1,024 cylinders. If a hard drive is being accessed by the BIOS and the physical drive contains more than 1,024 cylinders, then the BIOS presents an adjusted (logical) drive geometry with fewer than 1,024 cylinders by increasing the heads per cylinder value and decreasing the number of cylinders reported. In a DOS environment, a drive is usually accessed through the BIOS, but software can directly access the physical drive if the necessary device driver is available. For example, the Quantum Sirocco model 1700A has the direct physical and BIOS access parameters presented in Table 2-2.

Table 2-2. Example of Direct ATA versus BIOS Hard Drive Geometry

Access	Cylinders	Heads	Sectors per Head	Sectors per Cylinder	Total Sectors
Direct	3,309	16	63	1,008	3,335,472
BIOS	826	64	63	4,032	3,330,432

Note that 5,040 more sectors (3,335,472 minus 3,330,432) can be accessed through direct ATA than are reported by the legacy BIOS.

Test cases: DI-003, DI-048, DI-063, DI-064, DI-069, and DI-070.

2.2 Logical Restore Anomaly

For certain partition types (FAT32 and NTFS), a logical restore of a partition is not an exact duplicate of the original. The vendor documentation states that a logical restore cannot be verified as an exact copy of the source and is not recommended when seeking to create a bit-stream duplicate of the source. For FAT32 partitions, two file system control values (not part of any data file) are adjusted as a side effect of restoring an image to a destination. This adjustment is confined to about 8 bytes of sector 1 and the first sector of the FAT table (and FAT table backup copy) of the partition. For NTFS partitions, other changes were made to about 35 sectors of the partition. In no case was there any effect on sectors used in data files. All sectors of the image file accurately reflect the original sectors. These changes to a restored partition (logical volume) may be a consequence of the Windows shutdown process.

Test cases: DI-072, DI-089, DI-101, DI-108, DI-118, DI-130, and DI-147.

2.2.1 Logical restore anomaly mitigation

The **logical restore anomaly** appears to stem from the normal Windows 2000 shutdown process. A similar anomaly is discussed in a white paper on the vendor Web site, *Validation Testing of the EnCase Restore Process in Windows.*[1] During discussions with the vendor (and in the white paper), the suggestion was made to shut down the system by turning off the power without going through the normal shutdown procedure. Since powering off the entire system could compromise the integrity of other files on the system, NIST modified this procedure to power off only the destination drive and then follow the normal Windows 2000 shutdown procedure. The result of the modified procedure was to eliminate the anomaly from the restored copy while maintaining the integrity of the remainder of the file system. The modified procedure was used for test cases DI-084 and DI-145.

2.2.2 Sector change in FAT32 operation

In FAT32 restore operations, two changes to the destination were observed. The changes were adjustments to the **FSInfo** sector and the FAT table. The **FSInfo** sector (sector 1 of the

---

[1] *http://www.guidancesoftware.com/whitepapers/restorevalidation.shtm*

destination) differs by one byte beginning at offset 488 of sector 1 of the source. This **FSInfo** sector contains control information for the FAT32 file system.[2]

Table 2-3 is extracted from page 21 of *Microsoft Extensible Firmware Initiative FAT32 File System Specification FAT: General Overview of On-Disk Format* (see footnote 2).

Table 2-3. FAT32 FSInfo Sector Control Fields Modified by EnCase

Name	Offset (byte)	Size (bytes)	Description
FSI_Free_Count	488	4	Contains the last known free cluster count on the volume. If the value is 0xFFFFFFFF, then the free count is unknown and must be computed. Any other value can be used, but is not necessarily correct. It should be range checked at least to make sure it is <= volume cluster count.
FSI_Nxt_Free	492	4	This is a hint for the FAT driver. It indicates the cluster number at which the driver should start looking for free clusters. Because a FAT32 FAT is large, it can be rather time consuming if there are a lot of allocated clusters at the start of the FAT and the driver starts looking for a free cluster starting at cluster 2. Typically this value is set to the last cluster number that the driver allocated. If the value is 0xFFFFFFFF, then there is no hint and the driver should start looking at cluster 2. Any other value can be used, but should be checked first to make sure it is a valid cluster number for the volume.

For some of the FAT32 partition restore test cases in the first sector of both the primary copy and backup copy, the FAT table has a single byte change. The changes in the restored copy for test case DI-089 are presented in the following log file extracted from the **seccmp** program:

```
Compare sectors at: Src 64 (63+1) Dst 64 (63+1)
Src 480: 00 00 00 00 72 72 41 61 53 95 12 00 34 00 00 00
diff    :                                    **
Dst 480: 00 00 00 00 72 72 41 61 53 95 12 00 02 00 00 00
1 bytes different

Compare sectors at: Src 95 (63+32) Dst 95 (63+32)
Src   0: F8 FF FF 0F FF FF FF 0F F8 FF FF 0F 00 00 00 00
diff    :                       **
Dst   0: F8 FF FF 0F FF FF FF FF F8 FF FF 0F 00 00 00 00
1 bytes different
```

---

[2] This sector is documented in *Microsoft Extensible Firmware Initiative FAT32 File System Specification FAT: General Overview of On-Disk Format*. This document can be found on the Microsoft Web site: *http://www.microsoft.com/hwdev/download/hardware/FATGEN103.doc*.

```
Compare sectors at: Src 9611 (63+9548) Dst 9611 (63+9548)
Src   0: F8 FF FF 0F FF FF FF 0F F8 FF FF 0F 00 00 00 00
diff  :                        **
Dst   0: F8 FF FF 0F FF FF FF FF F8 FF FF 0F 00 00 00 00
1 bytes different
```

Sector 64 is the **FSInfo** sector; sector 95 is the first sector of the primary FAT table; Sector 9,611 is the first sector of the backup FAT table.

2.2.3 Sector change in NTFS logical restore operation

The execution of test case DI-084 using the modified shutdown procedure described in section 2.2.1 is presented in section 8, "Test Result Summaries." No sectors differ in the comparison between the source and the destination. Test case DI-084 was executed a second time using a normal Windows 2000 shutdown procedure. There were a number of differences between the original and the restored logical drive, as noted in the following extract from the partition compare log file:

```
Source base sector 10,249,533 Destination base sector 63
Sectors compared:      1,236,942
Sectors match:         1,236,906
Sectors differ:               36
Bytes differ:              2,548
Diffs range:  618,470-618,471; 618,480-618,498; 618,502-618,506;
618,510-618,517; 1,236,940-1,236,941
```

2.3 Restore Size Anomaly

A restore operation to an entire drive requires a destination drive larger than the source. In other words, an attempt to restore an entire drive to a drive of an identical size does not restore all sectors imaged from the source to the destination. Figure 2-1 is a screen capture for case DI-064, indicating that the destination drive is too small. The actual destination was identical in size to the source drive. This is documented on the EnCase Web site but not in the manual distributed with version 3.20. This anomaly was observed only in the Windows 2000 environment, not in the Windows 98 environment.

Figure 2-1. Warning Pop-Up Indicating Too Small Destination

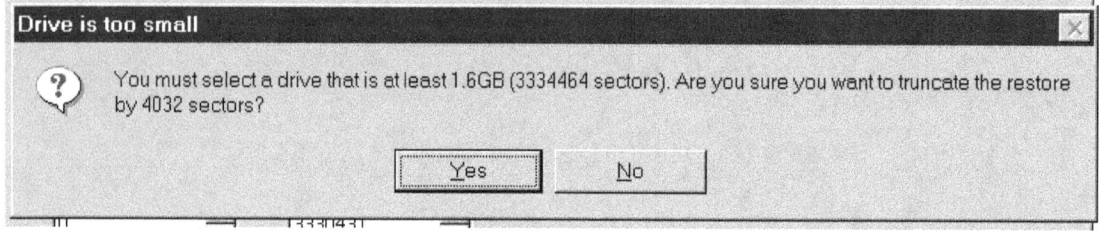

Test cases: DI-093, DI-098, DI-099, DI-122, DI-127, DI-128, DI-153, DI-161, and DI-164.

The **restore size anomaly** also effects filling of excess sectors. If restoring to a drive larger than the source with the *wipe excess sectors* option selected, then not all the excess sectors are wiped. This anomaly was observed only in the Windows 2000 environment, not in the Windows 98 environment.

Test cases: DI-045 and DI-060.

3.   Test Case Selection

Not all of the 168 test cases specified in *Disk Imaging Tool Specification, Version 3.1.6* apply to EnCase. Some test cases were modified so EnCase features that would not be tested otherwise could be included.

The primary criterion for selecting a test case is that there must be a tool feature covered by the objective of the test case as defined by the test case summary from *Disk Imaging Tool Specification, Version 3.1.6*. For example, test case DI-063 calls for the following setup: Image a BIOS-IDE source disk to a BIOS-IDE destination disk where the source disk is smaller than the destination. Since every parameter specified in the setup can be applied to EnCase, test case DI-063 is used. However, test case DI-113—imaging a Linux (i.e., ext2 or ext3) partition—is not used because EnCase does not allow selection of a Linux partition for the copy operation.

3.1 Inapplicable Test Cases

Test cases that met the following criteria were designated as not applying to EnCase testing:

- Some test cases assume a feature not supported by EnCase. These include copy operation, removable destination media, NTFS partitions (in DOS), and advanced SCSI programming interface (ASPI).
- Logical acquisition and restore of Linux EXT2 partitions were not tested.
- Some test cases are going to be deleted from the test specification and are not ever used to test any disk imaging tools. For example, cases involving deleted file recovery are being deleted from the specification because deleted file recovery tools will be tested separately.
- Some test cases require support software or other tools that are not available. For example, some test cases specify I/O error simulation beyond the scope of the current tools, such as destination write error or image read error in a Windows environment.
- Some of the corrupt image cases are redundant for EnCase.

Case	Reason Not Applied
DI-001	Copy operation.
DI-002	Copy operation.
DI-003	Copy operation.
DI-004	Copy operation.
DI-005	Copy operation.
DI-006	Copy operation, destination write.
DI-007	Copy operation.
DI-008	Copy operation.
DI-009	Copy operation.

Case	Reason Not Applied
DI-010	Copy operation.
DI-011	Copy operation.
DI-012	Copy operation.
DI-013	Copy operation, deleted case, Linux partition.
DI-014	Copy operation.
DI-015	Copy operation, destination write.
DI-016	Copy operation.
DI-017	Copy operation.
DI-018	Copy operation.
DI-019	Copy operation.
DI-020	Copy operation.
DI-021	Copy operation, destination write.
DI-022	Copy operation.
DI-023	Copy operation.
DI-024	Copy operation.
DI-025	Copy operation.
DI-026	Copy operation, deleted case.
DI-027	Copy operation.
DI-028	Copy operation, destination write.
DI-029	Copy operation.
DI-029	Linux partition.
DI-030	Copy operation.
DI-031	Copy operation.
DI-032	Copy operation.
DI-033	Copy operation.
DI-034	Copy operation, destination write.
DI-035	Copy operation.
DI-036	Copy operation.
DI-037	Copy operation, Linux partition.
DI-038	Copy operation.
DI-039	Copy operation, deleted case.
DI-040	Copy operation.
DI-041	Copy operation, destination write.
DI-042	Copy operation.
DI-043	Copy operation, Linux partition.
DI-044	Copy operation.
DI-045	Copy operation.
DI-046	Copy operation.
DI-047	Copy operation.
DI-048	Copy operation.
DI-049	Copy operation.
DI-050	Copy operation, ASPI.
DI-051	Copy operation, ASPI.
DI-052	Copy operation, ASPI.
DI-053	Copy operation, ASPI.
DI-054	Copy operation, ASPI.
DI-055	Copy operation, ASPI.
DI-056	Copy operation.
DI-057	Copy operation.
DI-058	Copy operation.
DI-059	Copy operation.
DI-060	Copy operation.
DI-061	Copy operation.
DI-065	Destination write.
DI-066	Image read.
DI-068	Redundant corrupt image.

Case	Reason Not Applied
DI-073	Removable media.
DI-074	Removable media, Linux partition.
DI-075	Deleted case.
DI-076	Deleted case.
DI-077	Removable media, deleted case.
DI-078	Removable media, deleted case, Linux partition.
DI-079	Linux partition.
DI-080	Destination write.
DI-081	Image read.
DI-084	NTFS.
DI-085	Removable media, image read, Linux partition.
DI-086	Removable media.
DI-087	Removable media.
DI-088	Removable media, Linux partition.
DI-090	Removable media.
DI-094	Destination write.
DI-095	Image read.
DI-096	Beyond scope of error simulator.
DI-097	Redundant corrupt image.
DI-102	Removable media.
DI-103	Removable media.
DI-103	Linux partition.
DI-104	Deleted case, Linux partition.
DI-105	Deleted case.
DI-106	Removable media, deleted case.
DI-107	Removable media, deleted case.
DI-109	Destination write.
DI-110	Image read.
DI-111	Linux partition.
DI-112	NTFS.
DI-113	Linux partition.
DI-114	Removable media, image read.
DI-115	Removable media.
DI-116	Removable media.
DI-117	Removable media, Linux partition.
DI-119	Removable media.
DI-123	Destination write.
DI-124	Image read.
DI-125	Beyond scope of error simulator.
DI-126	Redundant corrupt image.
DI-131	Removable media.
DI-132	Removable media, Linux partition.
DI-133	Deleted case.
DI-134	Deleted case.
DI-135	Removable media, deleted case.
DI-136	Removable media, deleted case, Linux partition.
DI-138	Destination write.
DI-139	Image read.
DI-143	Removable media, image read.
DI-144	Removable media.
DI-145	Removable media.
DI-146	Removable media.
DI-148	Removable media.
DI-151	Redundant corrupt image.
DI-154	ASPI.
DI-155	ASPI.

Case	Reason Not Applied
DI-156	ASPI.
DI-157	ASPI.
DI-158	ASPI.
DI-159	Redundant corrupt image.
DI-162	Redundant corrupt image.
DI-165	Copy operation, deleted case.
DI-166	Copy operation, deleted case.
DI-167	Deleted case.
DI-168	Deleted case.

3.2 Modified Test Cases

Several test cases were modified to increase the coverage of EnCase testing. The test cases in *Disk Imaging Tool Specification, Version 3.1.6* do not provide for the following:

- Acquisition of an image through an interface other than IDE or SCSI (e.g., FastBloc acquisition of an IDE drive via a SCSI interface in Windows).
- Filling of excess sectors after an image restore.
- Using direct ATA access to acquire an image and then restoring with a Windows interface.
- Cylinder alignment of a restored copy.

To address these issues, the following changes were made to selected test cases:

- Test cases DI-060, DI-084, and DI-112 were modified for inclusion with the source interface changed from **XBIOS-IDE** to **FastBloc** and the destination interface to Windows 2000.
- Test Case DI-145 was modified for inclusion with the operation changed from **image-rm** to **image**, the source interface changed to **XBIOS-SCSI,** and the destination interface changed to Windows 2000.
- Test Case DI-154 was modified for inclusion with excess sector fill turned on, the source interface changed to **XBIOS-SCSI,** and the destination interface changed to Windows 98.
- Test case DI-101 was modified to specify **Fill excess sectors** on the destination.
- Test cases DI-003, DI-019, DI-044, and DI-048 were modified for inclusion with the operation changed from **copy** to **image** and the destination interface to Windows 98.
- Test case DI-045 was modified for inclusion with the operation changed from **copy** to **image** and the destination interface to Windows 2000.
- Test cases DI-089, DI-150, DI-152, and DI-153 were modified to specify Windows 2000 for the destination interface.
- Test case DI-149 was modified to specify Windows 98 for the destination interface.
- In general, except as noted, a destination interface of **BIOS-IDE** was changed to Windows 98 and any **XBIOS** destination interface was changed to Windows 2000.

There were 50 test cases run (listed with modifications from the original version in *Disk Imaging Tool Specification, Version 3.1.6*). All test cases with the **Obj** parameter value of all are physical image and restores. All test cases with the **Obj** parameter value equal to a partition type (e.g., FAT16, etc.) are logical image and restores. The entries in the **Err** column indicate the type of error introduced as follows: src rd (source read), dst wt (destination write), img rd (image read), img wt (image weight), and corrupt (the image file has been changed).

Case	Src	Dst	Rel size	Err	Obj
DI-003	BIOS-IDE	Windows 98	Src < dst (n,a)	None	All
DI-019	XBIOS-IDE	Windows 98	Src < dst (f,n)	None	All
DI-044	DIRECT-IDE	Windows 98	Src < dst (n,n)	None	All
DI-045	DIRECT-IDE	Windows 2000	Src < dst (f,n)	None	All
DI-048	DIRECT-IDE	Windows 98	Src = dst	None	All
DI-060	FastBloc	Windows 2000	Src < dst (f,n)	None	All
DI-062	BIOS-IDE	Windows 98	Src < dst (n,n)	Corrupt	All
DI-063	BIOS-IDE	Windows 98	Src < dst (n,n)	None	All
DI-064	BIOS-IDE	Windows 98	Src = dst	Src rd	All
DI-067	BIOS-IDE	Windows 98	Src = dst	Img wt	All
DI-069	BIOS-IDE	Windows 98	Src = dst	None	All
DI-070	BIOS-IDE	Windows 98	Src > dst	None	All
DI-071	BIOS-IDE	Windows 98	Src < dst (n,n)	Corrupt	FAT16
DI-072	BIOS-IDE	Windows 98	Src < dst (n,n)	None	FAT32
DI-082	BIOS-IDE	Windows 98	Src = dst	Img wt	FAT16
DI-083	BIOS-IDE	Windows 98	Src = dst	Corrupt	FAT32
DI-084	FastBloc	Windows 2000	Src = dst	None	NTFS
DI-089	BIOS-IDE	Windows 2000	Src > dst	None	FAT32
DI-091	XBIOS-IDE	Windows 2000	Src < dst (n,n)	Corrupt	All
DI-092	XBIOS-IDE	Windows 2000	Src < dst (n,n)	None	All
DI-093	XBIOS-IDE	Windows 2000	Src = dst	Src rd	All
DI-098	XBIOS-IDE	Windows 2000	Src = dst	None	All
DI-099	XBIOS-IDE	Windows 2000	Src > dst	None	All
DI-100	XBIOS-IDE	Windows 2000	Src < dst (n,n)	Corrupt	FAT16
DI-101	XBIOS-IDE	Windows 2000	Src < dst (n,n)	None	FAT32
DI-108	XBIOS-IDE	Windows 2000	Src = dst	Src rd	FAT32
DI-112	FastBloc	Windows 2000	Src = dst	Corrupt	NTFS
DI-118	XBIOS-IDE	Windows 2000	Src > dst	None	FAT32
DI-120	XBIOS-SCSI	Windows 2000	Src < dst (n,n)	Corrupt	All
DI-121	XBIOS-SCSI	Windows 2000	Src < dst (n,n)	None	All
DI-122	XBIOS-SCSI	Windows 2000	Src = dst	Src rd	All
DI-127	XBIOS-SCSI	Windows 2000	Src = dst	None	All
DI-128	XBIOS-SCSI	Windows 2000	Src > dst	None	All
DI-129	XBIOS-SCSI	Windows 2000	Src < dst (n,n)	Corrupt	FAT16
DI-130	XBIOS-SCSI	Windows 2000	Src < dst (n,n)	None	FAT32
DI-137	XBIOS-SCSI	Windows 2000	Src = dst	Src rd	FAT16
DI-140	XBIOS-SCSI	Windows 2000	Src = dst	Img wt	FAT16
DI-141	XBIOS-SCSI	Windows 2000	Src = dst	Corrupt	FAT32
DI-142	XBIOS-SCSI	Windows 2000	Src = dst	None	FAT16
DI-145	XBIOS-SCSI	Windows 2000	Src = dst	None	FAT32
DI-147	XBIOS-SCSI	Windows 2000	Src > dst	None	FAT32
DI-149	DIRECT-IDE	Windows 98	Src < dst (n,n)	Corrupt	All
DI-150	DIRECT-IDE	Windows 2000	Src < dst (n,n)	None	All
DI-152	DIRECT-IDE	Windows 2000	Src = dst	None	All
DI-153	DIRECT-IDE	Windows 2000	Src > dst	None	All
DI-154	XBIOS-SCSI	Windows 98	Src < dst (n,f)	None	All
DI-160	XBIOS-IDE	Windows 2000	Src < dst (n,n)	None	All
DI-161	XBIOS-IDE	Windows 2000	Src > dst	None	All
DI-163	XBIOS-SCSI	Windows 2000	Src < dst (n,n)	None	All
DI-164	XBIOS-SCSI	Windows 2000	Src > dst	None	All

4. Test Results by Assertion

This section presents the results of EnCase 3.20 testing with results grouped by assertion. The assertions are taken from the *Disk Imaging Tool Specification, Version 3.1.6.*

4.1 Mandatory Assertions

AM-1.   If a source is accessed by the tool, then the source will not be altered.

After each source disk is created, a SHA-1 hash value is calculated and saved. Each time the tool is run, another SHA-1 hash value is calculated after the run and compared to the saved value. For all test cases that were run, the hash codes matched (i.e., the source was not altered).

The column labeled **Case** is the test case ID. **Before SHA-1** is the first four and last four digits (in hexadecimal) of the SHA computed on the source disk before running any test cases. **After SHA-1** is the first four and last four digits (in hexadecimal) of the SHA computed on the source disk after executing EnCase for the given test case. The **SHA Values Match?** column indicates whether the full hash values match.

Case	Before SHA-1	After SHA-1	SHA Values Match?
DI-003	D0FC ... 428F	D0FC ... 428F	OK
DI-019	83A0 ... 2A54	83A0 ... 2A54	OK
DI-044	D0FC ... 428F	D0FC ... 428F	OK
DI-045	8034 ... B235	8034 ... B235	OK
DI-048	D0FC ... 428F	D0FC ... 428F	OK
DI-060	8034 ... B235	8034 ... B235	OK
DI-062	3E7E ... C05A	3E7E ... C05A	OK
DI-063	D0FC ... 428F	D0FC ... 428F	OK
DI-064	D0FC ... 428F	D0FC ... 428F	OK
DI-067	D0FC ... 428F	D0FC ... 428F	OK
DI-069	D0FC ... 428F	D0FC ... 428F	OK
DI-070	D0FC ... 428F	D0FC ... 428F	OK
DI-071	D0FC ... 428F	D0FC ... 428F	OK
DI-072	3E7E ... C05A	3E7E ... C05A	OK
DI-082	D0FC ... 428F	D0FC ... 428F	OK
DI-083	3E7E ... C05A	3E7E ... C05A	OK
DI-084	8034 ... B235	8034 ... B235	OK
DI-089	B54E ... 2015	B54E ... 2015	OK
DI-091	3DE5 ... FD14	3DE5 ... FD14	OK
DI-092	83A0 ... 2A54	83A0 ... 2A54	OK
DI-093	83A0 ... 2A54	83A0 ... 2A54	OK
DI-098	83A0 ... 2A54	83A0 ... 2A54	OK
DI-099	83A0 ... 2A54	83A0 ... 2A54	OK
DI-100	83A0 ... 2A54	83A0 ... 2A54	OK
DI-101	3DE5 ... FD14	3DE5 ... FD14	OK
DI-108	3DE5 ... FD14	3DE5 ... FD14	OK
DI-112	8034 ... B235	8034 ... B235	OK
DI-118	3DE5 ... FD14	3DE5 ... FD14	OK
DI-120	0F9D ... 7AB0	0F9D ... 7AB0	OK
DI-121	25BF ... 9CBF	25BF ... 9CBF	OK
DI-122	25BF ... 9CBF	25BF ... 9CBF	OK
DI-127	25BF ... 9CBF	25BF ... 9CBF	OK
DI-128	25BF ... 9CBF	25BF ... 9CBF	OK

DI-129	0F9D ... 7AB0	0F9D ... 7AB0	OK
DI-130	25BF ... 9CBF	25BF ... 9CBF	OK
DI-137	0F9D ... 7AB0	0F9D ... 7AB0	OK
DI-140	0F9D ... 7AB0	0F9D ... 7AB0	OK
DI-141	25BF ... 9CBF	25BF ... 9CBF	OK
DI-142	0F9D ... 7AB0	0F9D ... 7AB0	OK
DI-145	25BF ... 9CBF	25BF ... 9CBF	OK
DI-147	25BF ... 9CBF	25BF ... 9CBF	OK
DI-149	3E7E ... C05A	3E7E ... C05A	OK
DI-150	83A0 ... 2A54	83A0 ... 2A54	OK
DI-152	83A0 ... 2A54	83A0 ... 2A54	OK
DI-153	83A0 ... 2A54	83A0 ... 2A54	OK
DI-154	0F9D ... 7AB0	0F9D ... 7AB0	OK
DI-160	FA03 ... 20B9	FA03 ... 20B9	OK
DI-161	FA03 ... 20B9	FA03 ... 20B9	OK
DI-163	25BF ... 9CBF	25BF ... 9CBF	OK
DI-164	6001 ... 5C9A	6001 ... 5C9A	OK

AM-2.   If there are no errors reading from a source or errors writing to a destination, then a bit-stream duplicate of the source will be created on the destination.

The column labeled **Case** is the test case ID. The type of object copied—disk or partition—is indicated in the **Obj** column. The column labeled **Src** is the number of sectors on the source to be copied. The column labeled **Dst** is the number of sectors on the destination. The number of sectors compared is listed in the **Compared** column. **Not Matched** indicates the number of sectors that were expected to compare equal but were different. The table is sorted first by type of object copied and then by case.

The **BIOS anomaly** is apparent (by values of 1,008; 5,040; and 4,032 in the **Not Matched** column). The **logical restore anomaly** is apparent as a value of 1 or 3 in the **Not Matched** column for the FAT32 test cases. The other non-zero **Not Matched** values (except for test case DI-084 discussed below) indicate the **Restore anomaly**.

Note that an initial examination of the results from test case DI-084 seems to imply an anomaly because the last two sectors of the partition did not match. This is not the case, because two more sectors are allocated to the physical NTFS partition than are actually used by the formatted NTFS file system. This can be verified by examining the number of sectors allocated to the NTFS file system. A value of 1,236,940 is reported as the number of allocated sectors, although the physical partition is actually two sectors larger. However, the partition compare program always compares the entire physical partition and for test case DI-084 compares two sectors too many. Those last two sectors of the physical partition are not germane to the test case because they are not used by the NTFS file system and are not imaged by EnCase during a logical acquire. However, those sectors are imaged by EnCase when performing a physical acquire of the entire disk.

Case	Obj	Src	Dst	Compared	Not Matched
DI-019	all	40188960	78177792	40188960	0
DI-044	all	3335472	12672450	3335472	0
DI-045	all	40188960	58633344	40188960	0
DI-048	all	3335472	3335472	3335472	5040
DI-060	all	40188960	58633344	40188960	0
DI-063	all	3335472	12672450	3335472	1008

Case	Obj	Src	Dst	Compared	Not Matched
DI-069	all	3335472	3335472	3335472	5040
DI-070	all	3335472	3173184	3173184	4032
DI-072	FAT32	1229697	1334529	1229697	1
DI-084	NTFS	1236942	1236942	1236942	2
DI-089	FAT32	1236942	1140552	1140552	3
DI-092	all	40188960	78177792	40188960	0
DI-098	all	40188960	40188960	40188960	10395
DI-099	all	40188960	39102336	39102336	126
DI-101	FAT32	1236942	1333332	1236942	3
DI-118	FAT32	1236942	1140552	1140552	3
DI-121	all	17938985	35885448	17938985	0
DI-127	all	17938985	17938985	17938985	10445
DI-128	all	17938985	17921835	17921835	9360
DI-130	FAT32	6152832	6361677	6152832	1
DI-142	FAT16	1236942	1236942	1236942	0
DI-145	FAT32	6152832	6152832	6152832	0
DI-147	FAT32	6152832	5943987	5943987	1
DI-150	all	40188960	58633344	40188960	0
DI-152	all	40188960	40188960	40188960	10395
DI-153	all	40188960	39102336	39102336	126
DI-154	all	17938985	35843670	17938985	1
DI-160	all	58633344	71687370	58633344	0
DI-161	all	58633344	35916548	35916548	11273
DI-163	all	17938985	39102336	17938985	0
DI-164	all	71687370	58633344	58633344	12159

AM-3.   If there are errors reading from a source or writing to a destination, then a qualified bit-stream duplicate of the source will be created on the destination. The identified areas are replaced by values specified by the tool's documentation.

The column labeled **Case** is the test case ID. The type of object copied is indicated in the **Obj** column. The type of error introduced is indicated in the **Err** column. **Not Matched** indicates the number of sectors that were expected to compare equal but were different. The **Range** column contains a list of sector ranges indicating contiguous blocks of sectors that do not match the expected results.

The **BIOS anomaly** is indicated in case DI-064. The **logical restore anomaly** is apparent as range values of 1, 32, and 9,548 in the **Range** column entry for case DI-108.

Case	Obj	Err	Not Matched	Range
DI-064	all	src rd	5041	40494, 3330432-3335471
DI-093	all	src rd	10446	1357-1407, 40178565-40188959
DI-108	FAT32	src rd	60	1, 32, 9548, 80711-80767
DI-122	all	src rd	10502	5938247-5938303, 17928540-17938984
DI-137	FAT16	src rd	7	145401-145407

AM-4.   If there are errors reading from the source or writing to the destination, then the error types and locations are logged.

The column labeled **Case** is the test case ID. The type of operation performed is indicated by the **Op** column. The type of error introduced is indicated in the **Err** column. The message from the

EnCase log file is in the **Message** column. The reported location (if any) is in the **Location** column.

Test cases DI-096 and DI-125 specify errors writing to an image file. Both cases produced a message indicating that the error occurred and that the image file could not be created.

Case	Op	Err	Message	Location
DI-064	image	src rd	blocks reported read errors	40448-40511
DI-093	image	src rd	blocks reported read errors	1344-1407
DI-108	image	src rd	blocks reported read errors	80704-80767
DI-122	image	src rd	blocks reported read errors	5938240-5938303
DI-137	image	src rd	blocks reported read errors	145344-145407

AM-5.   If the source or destination is an IDE or SCSI drive and an image or bit-stream duplicate is created, then the interface used is presumed to be well defined.[3]

See all test cases.

AM-6.   If the expected result of any test defined in this specification is achieved and the documentation was followed without change in achieving this result, then the documentation is presumed correct.

Some behavior of the tool was not well documented or was ambiguous.

AM-7.   If a bit-stream duplicate of a source is created on a larger destination, then the contents of areas on the destination that are not part of the duplicate are set to values as specified in the tool documentation.

The column labeled **Case** is the test case ID. The type of object copied is indicated in the **Obj** column. The **Do BF** column indicates that the EnCase backfill setting was selected. A value of *Yes* indicates that backfilling should be performed. The **Excess** column indicates the number of excess sectors on the destination. The number of excess sectors backfilled with user specified value is indicated in the **BF** column. The number of excess destination sectors that were not changed by EnCase is indicated in the **Not BF** column.

The **restore size anomaly** is apparent for test cases DI-045 and DI-060 by some sectors not being backfilled.

Case	Obj	Do BF	Excess	BF	Not BF
DI-019	all	yes	37988832	37988832	0
DI-044	all	no	9336978	0	9336978
DI-045	all	yes	18444384	18444384	12159
DI-060	all	yes	18444384	18444384	12159
DI-063	all	no	9336978	0	9336978
DI-072	FAT32	no	104832	0	104832
DI-092	all	no	37988832	0	37988832
DI-101	FAT32	yes	96390	96390	0
DI-121	all	no	17946463	0	17946463

---

[3] The actual assertion from the specification refers to a specific requirement. The essence of the referenced requirement is for the interface to be well defined.

Case	Obj	Do BF	Excess	BF	Not BF
DI-130	FAT32	no	208845	0	208845
DI-150	all	no	18444384	0	18444384
DI-154	all	yes	17904685	17904685	0
DI-160	all	no	13054026	0	13054026
DI-163	all	no	21163351	0	21163351

AM-8.   If a bit-stream duplicate of a source is created on a smaller destination, then the duplicate is qualified by omitted portions of the bit-stream, and the tool will notify the user that the source is larger than the destination.

The column labeled **Case** is the test case ID. The column labeled **Op** indicates the type of operation selected. The type of object copied is indicated in the **Obj** column. The message from a pop-up message box is in the **Message** column.

Case	Op	Obj	Message
DI-070	image	all	Drive is too small
DI-089	image	FAT32	Drive is too small
DI-099	image	all	Drive is too small
DI-118	image	FAT32	Drive is too small
DI-128	image	all	Drive is too small
DI-147	image	FAT32	Drive is too small
DI-153	image	all	Drive is too small
DI-161	image	all	Drive is too small
DI-164	image	all	Drive is too small

Figure 4-1 is a screen capture for case DI-118, where the destination is too small for the source.

Figure 4-1. Pop-up Message for DI-118

4.2 Optional Assertions

AO-1.   If a hash of one or more blocks (i.e., less than the entire disk) from the source is computed before duplication and is compared to a hash of the same blocks from the destination, the hashes will compare equal.

The column labeled **Case** is the test case ID. The type of operation is indicated in the **Op** column. The type of object copied is indicated in the **Obj** column. The type of error introduced is indicated in the **Err** column. The message from the log file is in the **Message** column.

The expected result for the corrupt (**Err**) entries is *could not be verified.*

Case	Obj	Err	Message
DI-003	all	none	Completely Verified, 0 Errors.
DI-019	all	none	Completely Verified, 0 Errors.
DI-044	all	none	Completely Verified, 0 Errors.

Case	Obj	Err	Message
DI-045	all	none	Completely Verified, 0 Errors.
DI-048	all	none	Completely Verified, 0 Errors.
DI-060	all	none	Completely Verified, 0 Errors.
DI-062	all	corrupt	integrity ... could not be verified:930752-930815
DI-063	all	none	Completely Verified, 0 Errors.
DI-064	all	src rd	Completely Verified, 0 Errors.
DI-067	all	img wt	Process terminated
DI-069	all	none	Completely Verified, 0 Errors.
DI-070	all	none	Completely Verified, 0 Errors.
DI-071	FAT16	corrupt	integrity ... could not be verified:16064-16127
DI-072	FAT32	none	Completely Verified, 0 Errors.
DI-082	FAT16	img wt	Process terminated
DI-083	FAT32	corrupt	integrity ... could not be verified:929920-929983
DI-084	NTFS	none	Completely Verified, 0 Errors.
DI-089	FAT32	none	Completely Verified, 0 Errors.
DI-091	all	corrupt	integrity ... could not be verified:32758528-32758591
DI-092	all	none	Completely Verified, 0 Errors.
DI-093	all	src rd	Completely Verified, 0 Errors.
DI-098	all	none	Completely Verified, 0 Errors.
DI-099	all	none	Completely Verified, 0 Errors.
DI-100	FAT16	corrupt	integrity ... could not be verified:16064-16127
DI-101	FAT32	none	Completely Verified, 0 Errors.
DI-108	FAT32	src rd	Completely Verified, 0 Errors.
DI-112	NTFS	corrupt	integrity ... could not be verified:1536-1599
DI-118	FAT32	none	Completely Verified, 0 Errors.
DI-120	all	corrupt	integrity ... could not be verified:4097088-4097151
DI-121	all	none	Completely Verified, 0 Errors.
DI-122	all	src rd	Completely Verified, 0 Errors.
DI-127	all	none	Completely Verified, 0 Errors.
DI-128	all	none	Completely Verified, 0 Errors.
DI-129	FAT16	corrupt	integrity ... could not be verified:16448-16511
DI-130	FAT32	none	Completely Verified, 0 Errors.
DI-137	FAT16	src rd	Completely Verified, 0 Errors.
DI-140	FAT16	img wt	Process terminated
DI-141	FAT32	corrupt	integrity ... could not be verified:4096512-4096575
DI-142	FAT16	none	Completely Verified, 0 Errors.
DI-145	FAT32	corrupt	integrity ... could not be verified:4096512-4096575
DI-147	FAT32	none	Completely Verified, 0 Errors.
DI-149	all	corrupt	integrity ... could not be verified:930432-930495
DI-150	all	none	Completely Verified, 0 Errors.
DI-152	all	none	Completely Verified, 0 Errors.
DI-153	all	none	Completely Verified, 0 Errors.
DI-154	all	corrupt	integrity ... could not be verified:4097088-4097151
DI-160	all	none	Completely Verified, 0 Errors.
DI-161	all	none	Completely Verified, 0 Errors.
DI-163	all	none	Completely Verified, 0 Errors.
DI-164	all	none	Completely Verified, 0 Errors.

For the 12 corrupt image file test cases, EnCase generates a message indicating that the image file has been corrupted somewhere within a range of sectors. The following table indicates the actual logical block address (LBA) location corrupted (**Corrupt Sector LBA**) and the range indicated by EnCase (**EnCase Range**). The column labeled **In Range** indicates whether EnCase correctly identified the location of the corrupted sector.

Case	Corrupt Sector LBA	EnCase Range	In Range
DI-062	930762	930752-930815	yes
DI-071	16065	16064-16127	yes
DI-083	929952	929920-929983	yes
DI-091	32758551	32758528-32758591	yes
DI-100	16065	16064-16127	yes
DI-112	1575	1536-1599	yes
DI-120	4097142	4097088-4097151	yes
DI-129	16486	16448-16511	yes
DI-141	4096575	4096512-4096575	yes
DI-145	4096575	4096512-4096575	yes
DI-149	930447	930432-930495	yes

AO-2.   If more than one partition exists on the source disk, the tool will produce a duplicate of any user-selected source partition on the destination.

FAT 16 partitions were copied correctly. FAT32 partitions were not always restored exactly. Using the normal system shutdown procedure, two fields—sector 1 of the partition and one entry in the FAT tables, both primary and backup—were modified. The fields contain file system control information. No data file content was affected by the change. For details, see section 2.2.2 "Sector change in FAT32 operation." Two test cases using an NTFS partition were acquired through the FastBloc device. For both NTFS and FAT32 partitions, the acquisition produced an accurate image file; however, an accurate restored copy could be produced only when the modified shutdown procedure described in section 2.2.1 was followed.

Results for the partition test cases are listed in the mandatory assertions section—FAT16 test cases: DI-071, DI-082, DI-100, DI-129, DI-137, DI-140, and DI-142; FAT32 test cases: DI-072, DI-083, DI-089, DI-101, DI-108, DI-118, DI-130, DI-141, DI-145, and DI-147; and NTFS test cases DI-084 and DI-112.

AO-3.   If a partition exists on the source, the tool will display or log a message indicating that the partition exists and display or log one or more items of information from the following list: drive indicator, device type, device address or mount point, size, space used, and free space.

No anomalies were observed.

AO-4.   If the tool logs the tool version, it will be the version referred to in the implementation's documentation.

No anomalies were observed.

AO-5. **If the subject disk identification is available and the tool is capable of logging the subject disk identification, then the subject disk identification will be logged.**

No anomalies were observed.

AO-6. **If the tool logs the source partition table in human-readable form and the information from the source partition table can be ascertained independently from the tool, then the source partition table information will accurately match the content of the independent partition table information.**

No anomalies were observed.

AO-7. **If the tool logs errors and any error occurs, then the type and location of the error will be logged.**

See AM-4.

AO-8. **If the tool logs tool actions and the tool's documentation states what actions are logged, then the actions logged will accurately match those documented in the tool's documentation.**

No anomalies were observed.

AO-9. **If the tool logs start and finish run times, then the logged start and finish run times will accurately match those recorded by the tester according to screen input images, test input scripts, or tester notes.**

No anomalies were observed.

AO-10. **If the tool logs tool settings and the tool's documentation states what settings are logged, then the logged settings will accurately match those set by the tester or documented in the tool's documentation.**

No anomalies were observed.

AO-11. **If the tool logs user comments, then the logged user comments will accurately match those entered by the tester as captured in screen input images, test input scripts, or tester notes.**

No anomalies were observed.

AO-12. **If the tool creates image files, then it will create an image file of a source on a magnetic medium that can be removed from the platform on which it was created.**

Magnetic tape removable media do not apply. Small (less than 250MB) media, such as floppy disks or zip disks, were not considered useful for imaging hard drives and were therefore not tested.

AO-13. **If the tool creates an image file from a source on a removable magnetic medium, then a duplicate of the source created from the removable magnetic medium will result in a duplicate on the destination, and the destination will compare equal to the source.**

Magnetic tape removable media do not apply. Small (less than 250MB) media, such as floppy disks or zip disks, were not considered useful for imaging hard drives and were therefore not tested.

AO-14. **If an image file is created, and there are no errors reading from a source or errors writing to a destination, then a bit-stream duplicate created from the image file will compare equal to the source.**

The results for image files are included in the results for the mandatory assertions and optional assertion AO-1.

5.   Testing Environment

The tests were run in the NIST CFTT lab. This section describes the hardware (i.e., test computers and hard drives) available for testing. Not all components were used in testing. The following host computers were available for executing test cases: Beta1, Beta3, Beta4, Beta6, Beta7, Delta1, Paladin, HecRamsey, McCloud, McMillin, AndWife, Cadfael, Rumpole, Wimsey, and JudgeDee. More than 35 hard drives (16 different models, 6 different brands) were used for the tests (Table 5-1). The tests were run with the hard drives arranged in one of several possible configurations (Table 5-4) as required by the test parameters.

5.1 Extended BIOS Host Computers

Four host computers (Cadfael, Rumpole, Wimsey, and JudgeDee) have the following hardware components in common:

Table 5-1. Extended BIOS Host Computer Hardware Components

```
ASUS CUSL2 Motherboard
BIOS: Award Medallion v6.0
Intel Pentium III (Coppermine) 933Mhz
512,672k Memory
Adaptec 29160N SCSI Adapter card
Plextor CR-RW PX-W124TS Rev: 1.06
Iomega 2GB Jaz drive Rev: E.17
LS-120 Super floppy
Two slots for removable IDE hard disk drives
Two slots for removable SCSI hard disk drive
```

Rumpole also had a 30GB OnStream SC30 tape drive (not used in the test procedures). JudgeDee had a third slot for a removable IDE hard disk drive.

Paladin, HecRamsey, McCloud, McMillin, and AndWife had the following hardware components in common:

Table 5-2. Alternate Extended BIOS Host Computer Hardware Components

```
Intel D845WNL Motherboard
BIOS: HV84510A.86A.0022.P05
Intel Pentium IV 2.0Ghz
512,672k Memory
Adaptec 29160 SCSI Adapter card
Tekram DC-390U3W SCSI Adapter card
Plextor CR-RW PX-W124TS Rev: 1.06
LG 52X CD-ROM
Floppy drive
Three slots for removable IDE hard disk drives
Two slots for removable SCSI hard disk drive
```

5.2 Legacy BIOS Host Computers

Beta1, Beta3, Beta4, Beta6 and Beta7 are Nexar 166MHz computers with 256MB RAM; two hard disk drive bays, both of which take hard drives mounted in removable carriages; a CD–ROM drive; a 1.44MB floppy drive; and a 17" color monitor. The motherboard is a HCL Hewlett-Packard Integrated ISA/PCI P54C with an Award v4.51PG BIOS. Beta7 also has an Adaptec 29160N SCSI Adapter card with an Iomega 2GB Jaz drive Rev: E.17 attached.

5.3 Fast SHA-1 for Nexar Tests

Delta1 is a Dell Computer Corporation system with 256MB RAM, one hard disk drive bay, one installed 15.37GB hard disk, a CD–ROM drive, a 1.44MB floppy drive, a 250MB zip drive, and a 17" color monitor. The BIOS is PhoenixBios 4.0 Release 6.0.

Delta1 is used to compute SHA-1 values for tests run on Nexar systems as needed. Delta1 (888Mhz) computes SHA-1 values much faster than the Nexar (166Mhz) systems.

5.4 Hard Disk Drives

The hard disk drives that were used were selected from the drives listed in Table 5-3. These hard drives were mounted in removable storage modules. Any combination of two IDE hard drives and two SCSI hard drives can be installed in Cadfael, Rumpole, Wimsey, and JudgeDee as required for a test. The legacy BIOS computers can have only two IDE drives mounted at a time.

The IDE disks used in the legacy BIOS computers have jumpers set manually to drive 0 for source drives and drive 1 for destination drives, and the media drive is set to either 0 or 1, depending on the available drive slot available after either the source or destination drive is installed. The IDE disks used in Cadfael, Rumpole, Wimsey, and JudgeDee have jumpers set for cable select.

The SCSI ID for the SCSI disk is set to either 0 or 1 as required by the test case. Except as noted, a source disk is set to ID 0, and a destination disk is set to ID 1.

Table 5-3. Hard Drives Available for Use in Testing

Label	Model	Interface	Usable Sectors	GB
11	FUJITSU MAN3184MC	SCSI	35,885,447	18.37
12	FUJITSU MAN3184MC	SCSI	35,885,447	18.37
1F	QUANTUM ATLAS10K3 18 SCA	SCSI	35,916,547	18.38
60	WDCWD64AA	IDE	12,594,960	6.44
61	WDCWD64AA	IDE	12,594,960	6.44
64	WDCWD64AA	IDE	12,594,960	6.44
70	IC35L040AVER07-0	IDE	80,418,240	41.17
75	IC35L040AVER07-0	IDE	80,418,240	41.17
7B	MAXTOR 6L040J2	IDE	78,177,792	40.02
7C	MAXTOR 6L040J2	IDE	78,177,792	40.02
91	WDC WD300BB-00CAA0	IDE	58,633,344	30.02
92	WDC WD300BB-00CAA0	IDE	58,633,344	30.02
93	WDC WD300BB-00CAA0	IDE	58,633,344	30.02
94	WDC WD300BB-00CAA0	IDE	58,633,344	30.02
9F	WDC WD200BB-32CFC0	IDE	39,102,336	20.02
A1	Quantum Sirocco 1700A	IDE	3,335,472	1.70
A4	Quantum Sirocco 1700A	IDE	3,335,472	1.70
A5	WDC WD200BB-00AUA1	IDE	39,102,336	20.02
A6	WDC WD200BB-00AUA1	IDE	39,102,336	20.02
A8	WDC WD200BB-00AUA1	IDE	39,102,336	20.02
B9	WDC AC21600H	IDE	3,173,184	1.62
CC	SEAGATE ST336705LC	SCSI	71,687,370	36.70
D3	Fujitsu MPE3064AT	IDE	12,672,450	6.48
D7	Quantum Sirocco 1700A	IDE	3,335,472	1.70
DA	Fujitsu MPE3064AT	IDE	12,672,450	6.48
DB	Fujitsu MPE3064AT	IDE	12,672,450	6.48
E1	QUANTUM ATLAS10K2-TY092J	SCSI	17,938,985	9.18
E2	QUANTUM ATLAS10K2-TY092J	SCSI	17,938,985	9.18
E3	QUANTUM ATLAS10K2-TY092J	SCSI	17,938,985	9.18
E4	QUANTUM ATLAS10K2-TY092J	SCSI	17,938,985	9.18
E6	SEAGATE ST318404LC	SCSI	35,843,670	18.35
EB	SEAGATE ST39204LC	SCSI	17,921,835	9.17
F1	Quantum Sirocco1700A	IDE	3,335,472	1.70
F5	IBM-DTLA-307020	IDE	40,188,960	20.57
F6	IBM-DTLA-307020	IDE	40,188,960	20.57
F7	IBM-DTLA-307020	IDE	40,188,960	20.57
F8	IBM-DTLA-307020	IDE	40,188,960	20.57

5.5 Test Configurations

The host computer and hard drive setup were determined by the test case parameters. Two or three disk drives were required for each test case. Except for corrupt image tests, source, destination, and media disks were required for all test cases. The corrupt image test cases did not require a destination drive. The source disk provided something to copy. The destination disk provided a place to put the copy. The media disk provided a place to put the image file for test cases that require the creation of an image file. The media disk also was used to provide the run-time Windows environment for running EnCase. One of two DOS boot floppies was selected and then used to create the run-time environment for the test case; the floppy contained control scripts and log files. A CD–ROM contained the support software and utility software. The support software provided for setup of test data, measurement of test results, and control of the test process.

The type of BIOS required for the test case determined the selection of the host computer. If an extended BIOS was required then either Paladin, HecRamsey, McCloud, McMillin, AndWife Cadfael, Rumpole, Wimsey, or JudgeDee was selected. If a legacy BIOS was required, then one of the Nexar computers was selected.

The factors determining the source disk selection were the source disk interface and type of source partition to use. A disk was selected with the matching interface and a partition of the type required for the test case. The factors for the selection of the destination drive were the destination interface and the relative size parameters. A drive was selected with the specified interface and, for whole disk copies, size relative to the source. For partition copies, the actual size of the destination drive did not matter because it was the size of the partition on the destination that was relevant. After the source and destination drives were selected, the media disk was selected for one of the two available drive slots.

The 12 system hard drive configurations used for the tests are presented in Table 5-4. The **Source** column indicates where the source drive was mounted. Only the primary IDE channel was used. The drive was usually positioned as drive 0. SCSI source drives were set to SCSI ID 0. The **Destination** column indicates the positioning of the destination drive. The **Media** column indicates the positioning of the media drive. The **Step** column indicates the phase of the test to which the configuration applies.

The media disk was swapped with either the source or destination disk as required for the step of the test case execution. If an image file was to be created, then only the source and media disk were installed. If the image was to be restored to the destination, then the source drive was replaced by the media drive. If the source was to be compared with the destination, then the media drive was not installed.

Table 5-4. System Configurations

ID	Step	Source	Destination	Media
1	Wipe		IDE primary 1	IDE primary 0
2	Wipe		SCSI ID 1	IDE primary 0
3	Acquire	IDE primary 0		IDE primary 1
4	Acquire	SCSI ID 0		IDE primary 0
5	Restore		IDE primary 1	IDE primary 0
6	Restore		SCSI ID 1	IDE primary 0
7	Compare	IDE primary 0	IDE primary 1	
8	Compare	IDE primary 0	SCSI ID 1	
9	Compare	SCSI ID 0	IDE primary 1	
10	Compare	SCSI ID 0	SCSI ID 1	
11	Hash	IDE primary 0		
12	Hash	SCSI ID 0		

5.6 Support Software

FS-TST Release 1.0 was developed to support the testing of disk imaging tools. FS-TST Release 1.0 can be obtained from *http://www.cftt.nist.gov*. The support software serves five main functions: initialization of a disk to a known value (DISKWIPE); comparison of a source with a destination (DISKCMP, PARTCMP, ADJCMP, and SECCMP); detection of changes to a disk (DISKHASH and SECHASH); corruption of an image file (CORRUPT); and simulation of a faulty disk (BADDISK and BADX13). All programs except for BADDISK and BADX13 were written in ANSI C and compiled with the Borland C++ compiler version 4.5. BADDISK and BADX13 were written in assembler language and compiled with Borland Turbo Assembler version 5.0.

For these test cases, version 3.2 of BADDISK and BADX13 was used, not the version 3.1 included in FS-TST Release 1.0. In addition to this software, one of two Windows 98 DOS boot floppies was used to create the run-time environment for the test case. The first floppy was used to create an environment to execute support software; the other boot floppy was created according to EnCase documentation and was used to provide the environment for source acquisition.

5.7 Basic Structure of Test Cases

A test case has five parts: setup, execution of the tool to acquire an image, execution of the tool to add the image to the case file, execution of the tool to restore the image to a destination drive, and measurement of the results. The setup for the test case was done in the DOS environment and involved the following steps:

1. Initialize a source disk to a known value.
2. Hash the source disk and save the hash value.
3. Initialize a destination disk to a known value.
4. If the test requires a partition on the destination, then create and format a partition on the destination disk.
5. If the test uses an image file, then partition and format a media disk. Also load either Windows 98 or Windows 2000 to the media disk and then install EnCase.

Note that steps 1, 2, and 5 are performed once and then used for several test cases.

Executing the support software required for each test tool being tested was done in the DOS environment. Except for NTFS partition acquisitions, all acquisitions were done in a DOS environment. All restore operations and NTFS acquisitions were done in a Windows environment. The steps in this execution phase were:

6. If the test requires a disk I/O error, then set up disk error simulation.
7. Use the tool to create an image file of the source on the media disk. This step was usually done in DOS; however, a few cases used FastBloc to acquire an image in the Windows 2000 environment. Note that where practical, the same image file was used for several test cases.
8. If the test requires a corrupted image file, then corrupt the image file.
9. Shutdown DOS and boot to Windows from the media disk.

10. Create a case file (i.e., for an investigation by the investigator) and use the **add evidence** function to add the image file to the case.
11. Use the disk imaging tool to create the destination disk by restoring an image file of the source to the destination. For corrupt image test cases, this step is omitted.

Measurement of the test results has three steps:

12. Compute a hash of the source disk and compare the computed hash value with the saved hash value. If the hashes are the same, then the tool has not altered the source disk.
13. If a destination is created, then compare the source to the destination to determine what sectors match and the disposition of any excess destination sectors.
14. Examine the tool log file for any expected messages. For example, in an I/O error test, there should be a message documenting the I/O error.

6. Test Results Summary Key

A summary of the actual test results is presented in this report. The following table presents a description of each section of the test results summary.

Heading	Description
First Line	Test case ID, Name and version of software tested.
Case Summary:	Test case summary from *Disk Imaging Tool Specification, Version 3.1.6.*
Tester Name:	Name or initials of person executing test procedure.
Test Date	Time and date that test was started.
PC:	Name of computer where tool under test was executed.
Disks:	Description of the hard disks used in the test as the source, destination, and media. The BIOS assigned drive number is in hexadecimal.
Source disk setup:	Documentation of the creation of the source disk including the disk label, the computer used for setup, person creating the source, time and date, partitions and operating systems installed, diskwipe command, and SHA-1 hash after the hard drive is configured.
Destination Setup:	Documentation of the creation of the destination disk including the diskwipe command. Note that for corrupt image test cases, a destination is not required.
Error Setup:	Support software commands executed to set up either an I/O error or to corrupt an image file.
Execute:	Documentation of each command executed during the test.
Log files & loc:	Name and location of the log files in the test file archive.
Log File Highlights:	Selected entries from three of the test case log files: • EnCase Report file. • Comparison of source and destination and for partition cases, the source and destination partition tables. • SHA-1 hash of the source drive after the test.
Expected Results:	Expected results listed in *Disk Imaging Tool Specification, Version 3.1.6.*

Heading	Description
Actual Results:	List of any anomalies observed.
Analysis:	Whether or not the expected results were achieved.

7.   Interpretation of Test Results

There are six main questions of interest when examining the results of a test case:

- Is the source disk unchanged?
- Has the correct number of sectors been accurately copied?
- Has the tool alerted the user to a destination smaller than the source?
- Has the tool handled excess destination sectors correctly as specified?
- Has the tool detected changes to an image file?
- Has the tool alerted the user to any I/O errors?

7.1 Source Disk

The integrity of the source disk is checked by comparing the hash of the source disk computed before any tests are run with the hash computed after the tool is used. If the two hash values are not the same, then there has been a change to the source disk by the tool. The reference hash is recorded in the **Source disk setup** box and the hash computed after the tool is run is recorded in the **Log file highlights** box.

7.2 Number of Sectors Copied

The number of sectors that should be copied is the minimum of the number of source sectors and the number of destination sectors. This value can be found on the *sectors compared* line of the **Log File Highlights** box. If the next line of the **Log File Highlights** box, *sectors differ*, is not zero, then the tool did not correctly copy all the sectors that should have been copied. The *LBAs* of the first few sectors not copied correctly are listed on the *diffs range* line.

The number of sectors in the source and destination can be determined as follows: If the tool operated on an entire disk, then the size of the source and destination can be found in the **Disks** box. If the tool operated on a single partition, then the partition sizes are presented in the *partition tables* in the **Log File Highlights** box. The partitions used in the test are identified in the /**select** option parameters to the **PARTCMP** program execution presented in the **Execute** box. The /**select** option is followed by two parameters: the partition numbers of the source and destination partitions.

7.3 Small Destination Detection

The tool should issue a message indicating that the destination is smaller than the source for any test case defined for a smaller destination. The message appears in a pop-up box on screen (see Figure 4-1 for an example) and is not logged to the EnCase report.

7.4 Excess Sectors

For disk operations, the tool should either backfill (set to user specified value) excess sectors or leave the contents as is. The tool action can be verified by the entries labeled *Zero fill, Other fill* and *Dst byte fill*, giving the count of sectors in each category. The number of excess sectors is indicated in the **Log File Highlights** box by the line with the text ". . . Source (. . .) has [number of excess sectors] fewer sectors . . . ."

7.5 Changes to an Image File

The **Error Setup** box presents the command used to change the image file and the absolute LBA of the corrupted sector. If the tool detects that the image file has been changed, the **Log File Highlights** box has a message indicating, "The integrity of the following sector groups could not be verified: . . . ."

The following table presents, for each corrupted image file test case, the original text in the image file (**Original**); the change, highlighted in bold (**Changed to**); the absolute LBA of the change (**Absolute LBA**); and for partition operations, the relative LBA of the corrupted sector (**Relative LBA**). For partition operations, EnCase reports the error location as an offset (relative LBA) from the beginning of the partition. The relative LBA is computed by subtracting the starting offset of the partition from the absolute LBA. For all cases except DI-112, the offset was 63. For test case DI-112, the offset was computed from the partition table of hard drive E4 (see test case DI-084). The offset is 63 + 8,193,150 + 2,056,320.

Case	Original	Changed to	Absolute LBA	Relative LBA
DI-062	923/006/01	92**Z**/006/01	930,762	No offset
DI-071	16/000/01	16/**9**00/01	16,128	16,065
DI-083	00922/010/10	00920/**8**10/10	930,015	929,952
DI-091	32498/009/01	32498/0**9**9/01	32,758,551	No offset
DI-100	16/000/01	16/0**7**0/01	16,128	16,065
DI-112	10169/012/01	10169/**8**12/01	10,251,108	1,575
DI-120	255/009/01	255/00**Q**/01	4,097,142	No offset
DI-129	1/007/44	1/0**7**7/44	16,549	16,486
DI-141	255/001/01	255/**Z**01/01	4,096,638	4,096,575
DI-145	255/001/01	255/**Z**01/01	4,096,638	4,096,575
DI-149	923/001/01	923/00**A**/01	930,447	No offset

7.6 I/O Errors

The **Error Setup** box presents the command used to setup an I/O error. If the tool detects the I/O error, the **Log File Highlights** box has a message indicating the type and location of the error.

8. Test Results Summaries

Case DI-003 for EnCase 3.20	
Case Summary:	Copy a BIOS-IDE source disk to a BIOS-IDE destination disk where the source disk is smaller than the destination and cylinder adjustment is turned on
Tester Name:	JRL
Test Date:	Sun Nov 10 09:14:33 2002
PC:	Beta3
Disks:	Source: DOS Drive 80 Physical Label A1 Destination: DOS Drive 81 Physical Label DA Image media: DOS Drive 80 Physical Label DB A1 is a Quantum Sirooco1700A with 3335472 sectors DA is a Fujitsu MPE3064AT with 12672450 sectors DB is a Fujitsu MPE3064AT with 12672450 sectors CD-ROM with PartitionMagic Pro 6.0 and boot floppy with run scripts FS-TST Release 1.0 CD-ROM + Baddisk 3.2 + Badx13 3.2
Source disk setup:	Linux EXT2 & DOS Fat16 Disk: A1 Host: JudgeDee Operator: JRL OS: Windows/Me Options: Typical Date: Tue Oct 16 11:24:16 2001 cmd: Z:\ss\DISKWIPE.EXE A1 JudgeDee 80 A1 /src /new_log X:\pm\pqmagic /cmd=X:\pm\nex-src.txt Load Operating System to Source disk cmd: Z:\ss\DISKHASH.EXE A1 JudgeDee 80 /before /new_log Disk hash = D0FC573FF774F6897BE520153C9BF770E998428F
Destination Setup:	Z:\ss\DISKWIPE.EXE DI-003 Beta3 81 DA /noask /dst /new_log /comment JRL No partition table defined
Error Setup:	none
Execute:	Z:\ss\DISKWIPE.EXE DI-003 Beta3 81 DA /noask /dst /new_log /comment JRL Z:\ss\DISKHASH.EXE DI-003 Beta3 80 /comment A1(JRL) /new_log /after
Log files loc:	test-archive/encase/encase-3.20/DI-003
Log File Highlights:	Image file acquired from DOS Restore environment Windows 98 EnCase report for case DI-003 is in DI-003.txt Evidence Number "A1-All" Alias "A1-All" File "D:\A1.E01" was acquired by JRL at 11/10/02 09:45:46AM. The computer system clock read: 11/10/02 09:45:46AM. Evidence acquired under DOS 7.10 using version 3.20. File Integrity: Completely Verified, 0 Errors. Verification Hash: 4385E645B15A9B9456C54CB4AE9640C8 Drive Geometry: Total Size 1.6GB (3,334,464 sectors) Cylinders: 827 Heads: 64 Sectors: 63

Partitions:

Code	Type	Start Sector	Total Sectors	Size
06	BIGDOS	0	1229760	600.5MB
83	Linux EXT2	2721600	64512	31.5MB
82	Linux Swap	2923200	411264	200.8MB
83	Linux EXT2	1431360	205632	100.4MB
06	BIGDOS	1636992	145152	70.9MB
16	HiddenFAT16	2193408	185472	90.6MB

Case DI-003 for EnCase 3.20	
	EnCase Report Case: DI-003 Page = = = = Measurement Logs = = = = Cylinder adjustment/alignment Summary Boot tracks 4 252 diffs 1 Partitions 6 2241540 diffs 3 Unallocated 5 1093680 diffs 1008 Total src sectors 3335472 Partition excess 0 zero 0 non-zero 0 Disk excess 9336978 zero 0 non-zero 9336978 Total dst sectors 12672450 Hash computed for this case (DI-003) Hash after test: D0FC573FF774F6897BE520153C9BF770E998428F
Expected Results:	Source disk is unchanged src compares qualified equal to dst
Actual Results:	BIOS anomaly
Analysis:	Expected results not achieved

Case DI-019 for EnCase 3.20	
Case Summary:	Copy an XBIOS-IDE source disk to an XBIOS-IDE destination disk where the source disk is smaller than the destination and sector fill is turned on
Tester Name:	JRL
Test Date:	Sun Nov 10 02:46:22 2002
PC:	McCloud
Disks:	Source: DOS Drive 80 Physical Label F5 Destination: DOS Drive 81 Physical Label 7B Image media: DOS Drive 80 Physical Label 91 F5 is an IBM-DTLA-307020 with 40188960 sectors 7B is a MAXTOR 6L040J2 with 78177792 sectors 91 is a WDC WD300BB-00CAA0 with 58633344 sectors CD-ROM with PartitionMagic Pro 6.0 and boot floppy with run scripts FS-TST Release 1.0 CD-ROM + Baddisk 3.2 + Badx13 3.2
Source disk setup:	Dual boot Linux/Windows Me with EXT2 & Fat16 Disk: F5 Host: Cadfael Operator: JRL OS: WindowsMe/Linux Date: Sat Aug 11 11:13:43 2001 DISKWIPE.EXE F5_SRC Cadfael 80 F5 /src X:\pm\pqmagic /cmd=X:\pm\fat-src.txt Load Operating System to Source disk DISKHASH.EXE F5_SRC Cadfael 80 /before Disk hash = 83A0002816BBF089F8BE33C41C92C3B5A0F42A54
Destination Setup:	Z:\ss\DISKWIPE.EXE DI-019 McCloud 81 7B /noask /dst /new_log /comment JRL No partition table defined
Error Setup:	none
Execute:	Z:\ss\DISKWIPE.EXE DI-019 McCloud 81 7B /noask /dst /new_log /comment JRL Z:\ss\DISKCMP.EXE DI-019 Cadfael 80 F5 81 7B /new_log /comment JRL Z:\ss\DISKHASH.EXE DI-019 Cadfael 80 /comment F5(JRL) /new_log /after
Log files loc:	test-archive/encase/encase-3.20/DI-019
Log File Highlights:	Image file acquired from DOS Restore environment Windows 98 EnCase report for case DI-019 is in 019.txt Evidence Number "F5-all" Alias "F5-all" File "D:\F5.e01" was acquired by JRL at 11/10/02 03:17:42AM. The computer system clock read: 11/10/02 03:17:42AM. Evidence acquired under DOS 7.10 using version 3.20. File Integrity: Completely Verified, 0 Errors. Verification Hash: 849BAEFDE9407109B9D22FBB479FE00D

Case DI-019 for EnCase 3.20

Drive Geometry:
Total Size   19.2GB (40,188,960 sectors)
Cylinders: 16,383
Heads: 16
Sectors: 63

Partitions:

Code	Type	Start Sector	Total Sectors	Size
06	BIGDOS	0	1237005	604.0MB
83	Linux EXT2	9430155	6152895	2.9GB
82	Linux Swap	39760875	417690	204.0MB
83	Linux EXT2	2249100	208845	102.0MB
06	BIGDOS	2457945	144585	70.6MB
16	HiddenFAT16	6699105	192780	94.1MB

EnCase Report
Case: DI-019   Page

= = = = Measurement Logs = = = =
Sectors Compared 40188960
Sectors Differ 0
Diffs range
Source (40188960) has 37988832 fewer sectors than destination
(78177792)
Zero fill: 37988832
Src Byte fill (F5):   0
Dst Byte fill (7B):   0
Other fill: 0
Other no fill: 0
Hash computed for this case (DI-019)
Hash after test: 83A0002816BBF089F8BE33C41C92C3B5A0F42A54

Expected Results:	Source disk is unchanged src compares qualified equal to dst
Actual Results:	No anomalies
Analysis:	Expected results achieved

Case DI-044 for EnCase 3.20

Case Summary:	Copy a direct access IDE source disk to a direct access IDE destination disk where the source disk is smaller than the destination
Tester Name:	JRL
Test Date:	Fri Jun 07 11:24:30 2002
PC:	Beta7
Disks:	Source: DOS Drive 80 Physical Label A1 Destination: DOS Drive 81 Physical Label DB Image media: DOS Drive 80 Physical Label D3 A1 is a Quantum Sirooco1700A with 3335472 sectors DB is a Fujitsu MPE3064AT with 12672450 sectors D3 is a Fujitsu MPE3064AT with 12672450 sectors CD-ROM with PartitionMagic Pro 6.0 and boot floppy with run scripts FS-TST Release 1.0 CD-ROM + Baddisk 3.2 + Badx13 3.2
Source disk setup:	Linux EXT2 & DOS Fat16 Disk: A1 Host: JudgeDee Operator: JRL OS: Windows/Me Options: Typical Date: Tue Oct 16 11:24:16 2001 cmd: Z:\ss\DISKWIPE.EXE A1 JudgeDee 80 A1 /src /new_log X:\pm\pqmagic /cmd=X:\pm\nex-src.txt Load Operating System to Source disk cmd: Z:\ss\DISKHASH.EXE A1 JudgeDee 80 /before /new_log Disk hash = D0FC573FF774F6897BE520153C9BF770E998428F

Case DI-044 for EnCase 3.20	
Destination Setup:	Z:\ss\DISKWIPE.EXE DI-044 Beta7 81 DB /noask /dst /new_log /comment JRL No partition table defined
Error Setup:	none
Execute:	Z:\ss\DISKWIPE.EXE DI-044 Beta7 81 DB /noask /dst /new_log /comment JRL Z:\ss\DISKCMP.EXE DI-044 Beta7 80 A1 81 DB /new_log /comment JRL Z:\ss\DISKHASH.EXE DI-044 Beta7 80 /comment A1(JRL) /new_log /after
Log files loc:	test-archive/encase/encase-3.20/DI-044
Log File Highlights:	Image file acquired from DOS Restore environment Windows 98 EnCase report for case DI-044 is in A1-ATA.txt Evidence Number "A1-ATA-1" Alias "A1-ATA-1" File "D:\A1-ata.e01" was acquired by JRL at 06/03/02 01:57:25PM. The computer system clock read: 06/03/02 01:57:25PM. Evidence acquired under DOS 7.10 using version 3.20. File Integrity: Completely Verified, 0 Errors. Verification Hash: 4A8A3498BFD4509ED7EA01B88119DE95 Drive Geometry: 	Total Size	1.6GB (3,335,472 sectors)
Cylinders:	3,309
Heads:	16
Sectors:	63 | Partitions: | Code	Type	Start Sector	Total Sectors	Size
---	---	---	---	---
06	BIGDOS	0	1229760	600.5MB
83	Linux EXT2	2721600	64512	31.5MB
82	Linux Swap	2923200	411264	200.8MB
83	Linux EXT2	1431360	205632	100.4MB
06	BIGDOS	1636992	145152	70.9MB
16	HiddenFAT16	2193408	185472	90.6MB	 EnCase Report Case: a1-ata Page = = = = Measurement Logs = = = = Sectors Compared 3335472 Sectors Differ 0 Diffs range Source (3335472) has 9336978 fewer sectors than destination (12672450) Zero fill: 0 Src Byte fill (A1): 0 Dst Byte fill (DB): 9336978 Other fill: 0 Other no fill: 0 Hash computed for this case (DI-044) Hash after test: D0FC573FF774F6897BE520153C9BF770E998428F
Expected Results:	Source disk is unchanged src compares qualified equal to dst
Actual Results:	No anomalies
Analysis:	Expected results achieved

Case DI-045 for EnCase 3.20	
Case Summary:	Copy a direct access IDE source disk to a direct access IDE destination disk where the source disk is smaller than the destination and sector fill is turned on
Tester Name:	JRL
Test Date:	Thu Nov 07 11:11:10 2002
PC:	AndWife
Disks:	Source: DOS Drive 80 Physical Label F6

	Destination: DOS Drive 81 Physical Label 91 Image media: DOS Drive 80 Physical Label 75 F6 is an IBM-DTLA-307020 with 40188960 sectors 91 is a WDC WD300BB-00CAA0 with 58633344 sectors 75 is a IC35L040AVER07-0 with 80418240 sectors CD-ROM with PartitionMagic Pro 6.0 and boot floppy with run scripts FS-TST Release 1.0 CD-ROM + Baddisk 3.2 + Badx13 3.2
Source disk setup:	Windows 2000 with NTFS & Fat32 Disk: F6 Host: Wimsey Operator: JRL OS: Windows 2000 Date: Sat Jul 21 15:53:12 2001 DISKWIPE.EXE F6_SRC Wimsey 80 F6 /src /new_log /noask /comment Windows 2000/NT source X:\pm\pqmagic /cmd=X:\pm\nt-src.txt Load Operating System to Source disk DISKHASH.EXE LX-27 Morse 80 /before Disk hash = 8034683D5D55BA51409AC7B5CB0845CA2CF6B235
Destination Setup:	Z:\ss\DISKWIPE.EXE DI-045 AndWife 81 91 /noask /dst /new_log /comment JRL No partition table defined
Error Setup:	none
Execute:	Z:\ss\DISKWIPE.EXE DI-045 AndWife 81 91 /noask /dst /new_log /comment JRL Z:\ss\DISKCMP.EXE DI-045 AndWife 80 F6 81 91 /new_log /comment JRL Z:\ss\DISKHASH.EXE DI-045 Rumpole 80 /comment F6(JRL) /new_log /after
Log files loc:	test-archive/encase/encase-3.20/DI-045
Log File Highlights:	Image file acquired from DOS Restore environment Windows 2000 EnCase report for case DI-045 is in 045.txt Evidence Number "F6-all" Alias "F6-all" File "D:\F6.E01" was acquired by JRL at 11/07/02 11:36:46AM. The computer system clock read: 11/07/02 11:36:46AM. Evidence acquired under DOS 7.10 using version 3.20. File Integrity: Completely Verified, 0 Errors. Verification Hash: 53682AAD75AE5EAD72F60BD9B3A55D2A Drive Geometry: Total Size 19.2GB (40,188,960 sectors) Cylinders: 16,383 Heads: 16 Sectors: 63

Partitions:

Code	Type	Start Sector	Total Sectors	Size
0B	FAT32	0	6152895	2.9GB
07	NTFS	10249470	1237005	604.0MB
17	Hidden IFS	13542795	1638630	800.1MB
1B	HiddenFAT32	38941560	1237005	604.0MB

EnCase Report
Case: DI-045   Page

= = = = Measurement Logs = = = =
Sectors Compared 40188960
Sectors Differ 0
Diffs range
Source (40188960) has 18444384 fewer sectors than destination
(58633344)

Case DI-045 for EnCase 3.20

	Zero fill: 18432225
	Src Byte fill (F6): 0
	Dst Byte fill (91): 12159
	Other fill: 0
	Other no fill: 0
	Hash computed for this case (DI-045)
	Hash after test: 8034683D5D55BA51409AC7B5CB0845CA2CF6B235
Expected Results:	Source disk is unchanged src compares qualified equal to dst
Actual Results:	Restore anomaly
Analysis:	Expected results not achieved

Case DI-048 for EnCase 3.20

Case Summary:	Copy a direct access IDE source disk to a direct access IDE destination disk where the source disk is the same size as the destination
Tester Name:	JRL
Test Date:	Fri Jun 07 11:15:21 2002
PC:	Beta3
Disks:	Source: DOS Drive 80 Physical Label A1 Destination: DOS Drive 81 Physical Label A4 Image media: DOS Drive 80 Physical Label D3 A1 is a Quantum Sirooco1700A with 3335472 sectors A4 is a Quantum Sirooco1700A with 3335472 sectors D3 is a Fujitsu MPE3064AT with 12672450 sectors CD-ROM with PartitionMagic Pro 6.0 and boot floppy with run scripts FS-TST Release 1.0 CD-ROM + Baddisk 3.2 + Badx13 3.2
Source disk setup:	Linux EXT2 & DOS Fat16 Disk: A1 Host: JudgeDee Operator: JRL OS: Windows/Me Options: Typical Date: Tue Oct 16 11:24:16 2001 cmd: Z:\ss\DISKWIPE.EXE A1 JudgeDee 80 A1 /src /new_log X:\pm\pqmagic /cmd=X:\pm\nex-src.txt Load Operating System to Source disk cmd: Z:\ss\DISKHASH.EXE A1 JudgeDee 80 /before /new_log Disk hash = D0FC573FF774F6897BE520153C9BF770E998428F
Destination Setup:	Z:\ss\DISKWIPE.EXE DI-048 Beta3 81 A4 /noask /dst /new_log /comment JRL No partition table defined
Error Setup:	none
Execute:	Z:\ss\DISKWIPE.EXE DI-048 Beta3 81 A4 /noask /dst /new_log /comment JRL Z:\ss\DISKCMP.EXE DI-048 Beta7 80 A1 81 A4 /new_log /comment JRL
Log files loc:	test-archive/encase/encase-3.20/DI-048
Log File Highlights:	Image file acquired from DOS Restore environment Windows 98 EnCase report for case DI-048 is in A1-ATA.txt Evidence Number "A1-ATA-1" Alias "A1-ATA-1" File "D:\A1-ata.e01" was acquired by JRL at 06/03/02 01:57:25PM. The computer system clock read: 06/03/02 01:57:25PM. Evidence acquired under DOS 7.10 using version 3.20. File Integrity: Completely Verified, 0 Errors. Verification Hash: 4A8A3498BFD4509ED7EA01B88119DE95 Drive Geometry: Total Size 1.6GB (3,335,472 sectors) Cylinders: 3,309 Heads: 16 Sectors: 63 Partitions:

Case DI-048 for EnCase 3.20

	Code	Type	Start Sector	Total Sectors	Size
	06	BIGDOS	0	1229760	600.5MB
	83	Linux EXT2	2721600	64512	31.5MB
	82	Linux Swap	2923200	411264	200.8MB
	83	Linux EXT2	1431360	205632	100.4MB
	06	BIGDOS	1636992	145152	70.9MB
	16	HiddenFAT16	2193408	185472	90.6MB

	EnCase Report Case: a1-ata Page = = = = Measurement Logs = = = = Sectors Compared 3335472 Sectors Differ 5040 Diffs range 3330432-3335471 This case uses the hash computed from case DI-044 Hash after test: D0FC573FF774F6897BE520153C9BF770E998428F
Expected Results:	Source disk is unchanged src compares equal to dst
Actual Results:	BIOS Anomaly
Analysis:	Expected results not achieved

Case DI-060 for EnCase 3.20

Case Summary:	Copy an XBIOS-SCSI source disk to an XBIOS-IDE destination disk where the source disk is smaller than the destination and sector fill is turned on
Tester Name:	JRL
Test Date:	Mon Nov 04 13:08:08 2002
PC:	AndWife
Disks:	Source: DOS Drive 80 Physical Label F6 Destination: DOS Drive 81 Physical Label 92 Image media: DOS Drive 80 Physical Label 75 F6 is an IBM-DTLA-307020 with 40188960 sectors 92 is a WDC WD300BB-00CAA0 with 58633344 sectors 75 is a IC35L040AVER07-0 with 80418240 sectors CD-ROM with PartitionMagic Pro 6.0 and boot floppy with run scripts FS-TST Release 1.0 CD-ROM + Baddisk 3.2 + Badx13 3.2
Source disk setup:	Windows 2000 with NTFS & Fat32 Disk: F6 Host: Wimsey Operator: JRL OS: Windows 2000 Date: Sat Jul 21 15:53:12 2001 DISKWIPE.EXE F6_SRC Wimsey 80 F6 /src /new_log /noask /comment Windows 2000/NT source X:\pm\pqmagic /cmd=X:\pm\nt-src.txt Load Operating System to Source disk DISKHASH.EXE LX-27 Morse 80 /before Disk hash = 8034683D5D55BA51409AC7B5CB0845CA2CF6B235
Destination Setup:	Z:\ss\DISKWIPE.EXE DI-060 AndWife 81 92 /noask /dst /new_log /comment JRL No partition table defined
Error Setup:	none
Execute:	Z:\ss\DISKWIPE.EXE DI-060 AndWife 81 92 /noask /dst /new_log /comment JRL Z:\ss\DISKCMP.EXE DI-060 AndWife 80 F6 81 92 /new_log /comment JRL Z:\ss\DISKHASH.EXE DI-060 AndWife 80 /comment F6(JRL) /new_log /after
Log files loc:	test-archive/encase/encase-3.20/DI-060
Log File Highlights:	Image file acquired from FastBloc Restore environment Windows 2000 EnCase report for case DI-060 is in 060.txt Evidence Number "F6" Alias "F6" File "D:\F6.E01" was acquired by JRL at 11/04/02 11:37:42AM.

Case DI-060 for EnCase 3.20

The computer system clock read: 11/04/02 11:38:00AM.

Evidence acquired under Windows 2000 using version 3.20. Hardware
Write-Blocker Enabled.

File Integrity:
Completely Verified, 0 Errors.
Verification Hash: 53682AAD75AE5EAD72F60BD9B3A55D2A

Drive Geometry:
Total Size   19.2GB (40,188,960 sectors)

Partitions:

Code	Type	Start Sector	Total Sectors	Size
0B	FAT32	0	6152895	2.9GB
07	NTFS	10249470	1237005	604.0MB
17	Hidden IFS	13542795	1638630	800.1MB
1B	HiddenFAT32	38941560	1237005	604.0MB

EnCase Report
Case: DI-060   Page

= = = = Measurement Logs = = = =
Sectors Compared 40188960
Sectors Differ 0
Diffs range
Source (40188960) has 18444384 fewer sectors than destination
(58633344)
Zero fill: 18432225
Src Byte fill (F6):   0
Dst Byte fill (92):   12159
Other fill: 0
Other no fill: 0
Hash computed for this case (DI-060)
Hash after test: 8034683D5D55BA51409AC7B5CB0845CA2CF6B235

Expected Results:	Source disk is unchanged src compares qualified equal to dst
Actual Results:	Restore anomaly
Analysis:	Expected results not achieved

Case DI-062 for EnCase 3.20

Case Summary:	Create an image from a BIOS-IDE source disk to a BIOS-IDE destination disk where the source disk is smaller than the destination Introduce an error on the image.
Tester Name:	JRL
Test Date:	Fri Aug 30 08:49:52 2002
PC:	Beta3
Disks:	Source: DOS Drive 80 Physical Label F1 Destination: DOS Drive 81 Physical Label none Image media: DOS Drive 80 Physical Label D3 F1 is a Quantum Sirooco1700A with 3335472 sectors D3 is a Fujitsu MPE3064AT with 12672450 sectors CD-ROM with PartitionMagic Pro 6.0 and boot floppy with run scripts FS-TST Release 1.0 CD-ROM + Baddisk 3.2 + Badx13 3.2
Source disk setup:	Linux EXT2 & Fat32 Disk: F1 Host: JudgeDee Operator: JRL OS: Windows/Me Options: Typical Date: Fri Nov 16 10:42:33 2001 cmd: Z:\ss\DISKWIPE.EXE F1 JudgeDee 80 F1 /src /new_log X:\pm\pqmagic /cmd=X:\pm\f32-src.txt Load Operating System to Source disk cmd: Z:\ss\DISKHASH.EXE F1 JudgeDee 80 /before /new_log

Case DI-062 for EnCase 3.20	
	Disk hash = 3E7E5E0AB0FA333BE39D267F0DB8E340386DC05A
Destination Setup:	No destination setup required
Error Setup:	cmd: Z:\ss\CORRUPT.EXE DI-062 Beta3 D:\F1.E01 476381896 5A Comment: CHange 923/006/01 to 92Z/006/01 at LBA 930762??
Execute:	Z:\ss\DISKHASH.EXE DI-062 Beta7 80 /comment F1(JRL) /new_log /after
Log files loc:	test-archive/encase/encase-3.20/DI-062
Log File Highlights:	Image file acquired from DOS Restore environment Windows 98 EnCase report for case DI-062 is in 062.txt Evidence Number "F1" Alias "F1" File "D:\F1.e01" was acquired by JRL at 08/30/02 09:10:20AM. The computer system clock read: 08/30/02 09:10:20AM. Evidence acquired under DOS 7.10 using version 3.20. The integrity of the following sector groups could not be verified:930752-930815 Drive Geometry: Total Size 1.6GB (3,334,464 sectors) Cylinders: 827 Heads: 64 Sectors: 63 Partitions: EnCase Report Case: di-062cas Page = = = = Measurement Logs = = = = No compare log found for DI-062 Hash computed for this case (DI-062) Hash after test: 3E7E5E0AB0FA333BE39D267F0DB8E340386DC05A
Expected Results:	Source disk is unchanged image verification error
Actual Results:	BIOS anomoly
Analysis:	Expected results not achieved

Partitions:

Code	Type	Start Sector	Total Sectors	Size
0B	FAT32	0	1229760	600.5MB
83	Linux EXT2	2721600	64512	31.5MB
82	Linux Swap	2923200	411264	200.8MB
83	Linux EXT2	1431360	205632	100.4MB
0B	FAT32	1636992	145152	70.9MB
16	HiddenFAT16	2193408	185472	90.6MB

Case DI-063 for EnCase 3.20	
Case Summary:	Create an image from a BIOS-IDE source disk to a BIOS-IDE destination disk where the source disk is smaller than the destination
Tester Name:	JRL
Test Date:	Sat May 25 17:28:49 2002
PC:	Beta3
Disks:	Source: DOS Drive 80 Physical Label A1 Destination: DOS Drive 81 Physical Label DB Image media: DOS Drive 80 Physical Label D3 A1 is a Quantum Sirooco1700A with 3335472 sectors DB is a Fujitsu MPE3064AT with 12672450 sectors D3 is a Fujitsu MPE3064AT with 12672450 sectors CD-ROM with PartitionMagic Pro 6.0 and boot floppy with run scripts FS-TST Release 1.0 CD-ROM + Baddisk 3.2 + Badx13 3.2
Source disk setup:	Linux EXT2 & DOS Fat16 Disk: A1 Host: JudgeDee Operator: JRL

	OS: Windows/Me Options: Typical Date: Tue Oct 16 11:24:16 2001 cmd: Z:\ss\DISKWIPE.EXE A1 JudgeDee 80 A1 /src /new_log X:\pm\pqmagic /cmd=X:\pm\nex-src.txt Load Operating System to Source disk cmd: Z:\ss\DISKHASH.EXE A1 JudgeDee 80 /before /new_log Disk hash = D0FC573FF774F6897BE520153C9BF770E998428F
Destination Setup:	Z:\ss\DISKWIPE.EXE DI-063 Beta3 81 DB /noask /dst /new_log /comment JRL No partition table defined
Error Setup:	none
Execute:	Z:\ss\DISKWIPE.EXE DI-063 Beta3 81 DB /noask /dst /new_log /comment JRL Z:\ss\DISKCMP.EXE DI-063 beta7 80 A1 81 DB /new_log /comment JRL
Log files loc:	test-archive/encase/encase-3.20/DI-063
Log File Highlights:	Image file acquired from DOS Restore environment Windows 98 EnCase report for case DI-063 is in a1-069.txt Evidence Number "1" Alias "1" File "D:\A1.e01" was acquired by jrl at 05/24/02 08:42:36AM. The computer system clock read: 05/24/02 08:42:36AM. Evidence acquired under DOS 7.10 using version 3.20. File Integrity: Completely Verified, 0 Errors. Verification Hash: 4385E645B15A9B9456C54CB4AE9640C8 Drive Geometry: Total Size 1.6GB (3,334,464 sectors) Cylinders: 827 Heads: 64 Sectors: 63 Partitions: Partitions table below EnCase Report Case: A1 Page = = = = Measurement Logs = = = = Sectors Compared 3335472 Sectors Differ 1008 Diffs range 3334464-3335471 Source (3335472) has 9336978 fewer sectors than destination (12672450) Zero fill: 0 Src Byte fill (A1): 0 Dst Byte fill (DB): 9336978 Other fill: 0 Other no fill: 0 This case uses the hash computed from case DI-069 Hash after test: D0FC573FF774F6897BE520153C9BF770E998428F
Expected Results:	Source disk is unchanged src compares qualified equal to dst
Actual Results:	BIOS Anomaly
Analysis:	Expected results not achieved

Partitions:

Code	Type	Start Sector	Total Sectors	Size
06	BIGDOS	0	1229760	600.5MB
83	Linux EXT2	2721600	64512	31.5MB
82	Linux Swap	2923200	411264	200.8MB
83	Linux EXT2	1431360	205632	100.4MB
06	BIGDOS	1636992	145152	70.9MB
16	HiddenFAT16	2193408	185472	90.6MB

Case DI-064 for EnCase 3.20	
Case Summary:	Create an image from a BIOS-IDE source disk to a BIOS-IDE destination disk where the source disk is the same size as the destination Introduce a read error from the source.
Tester Name:	JRL
Test Date:	Thu Sep 05 14:58:08 2002
PC:	Beta3
Disks:	Source: DOS Drive 80 Physical Label A1 Destination: DOS Drive 81 Physical Label A4 Image media: DOS Drive 80 Physical Label D3 A1 is a Quantum Sirooco1700A with 3335472 sectors A4 is a Quantum Sirooco1700A with 3335472 sectors D3 is a Fujitsu MPE3064AT with 12672450 sectors CD-ROM with PartitionMagic Pro 6.0 and boot floppy with run scripts FS-TST Release 1.0 CD-ROM + Baddisk 3.2 + Badx13 3.2
Source disk setup:	Linux EXT2 & DOS Fat16 Disk: A1 Host: JudgeDee Operator: JRL OS: Windows/Me Options: Typical Date: Tue Oct 16 11:24:16 2001 cmd: Z:\ss\DISKWIPE.EXE A1 JudgeDee 80 A1 /src /new_log X:\pm\pqmagic /cmd=X:\pm\nex-src.txt Load Operating System to Source disk cmd: Z:\ss\DISKHASH.EXE A1 JudgeDee 80 /before /new_log Disk hash = D0FC573FF774F6897BE520153C9BF770E998428F
Destination Setup:	Z:\ss\DISKWIPE.EXE DI-064 Beta3 81 A4 /noask /dst /new_log /comment JRL No partition table defined
Error Setup:	Z:\ss\baddisk 80 10 2 33 2 10 > a:\err-064.txt Z:\ss\baddisk 80 10 2 33 10 10 >> a:\err-064.txt return code 00010 on command 00002 from disk 00080 at address 00010/00002/00033 return code 00010 on command 00010 from disk 00080 at address 00010/00002/00033
Execute:	Z:\ss\DISKWIPE.EXE DI-064 Beta3 81 A4 /noask /dst /new_log /comment JRL Z:\ss\DISKCMP.EXE DI-064 Beta3 80 A1 81 A4 /new_log /comment JRL Z:\ss\DISKHASH.EXE DI-064 JudgeDee 80 /comment A1(JRL) /new_log /after
Log files loc:	test-archive/encase/encase-3.20/DI-064
Log File Highlights:	Image file acquired from DOS Restore environment Windows 98 EnCase report for case DI-064 is in 064.txt Evidence Number "A1-all" Alias "A1-all" File "D:\A1-err.e01" was acquired by JRL at 09/05/02 03:26:20PM. The computer system clock read: 09/05/02 03:26:20PM. Evidence acquired under DOS 7.10 using version 3.20. File Integrity: Completely Verified, 0 Errors. Verification Hash: 050B6F5A205D3EEB678B7FE562684F99 The following sector blocks reported read errors during acquisition: 40448-40511 Drive Geometry: Total Size 1.6GB (3,334,464 sectors) Cylinders: 827 Heads: 64 Sectors: 63

Case DI-064 for EnCase 3.20

	Partitions:				
	Code	Type	Start Sector	Total Sectors	Size
	06	BIGDOS	0	1229760	600.5MB
	83	Linux EXT2	2721600	64512	31.5MB
	82	Linux Swap	2923200	411264	200.8MB
	83	Linux EXT2	1431360	205632	100.4MB
	06	BIGDOS	1636992	145152	70.9MB
	16	HiddenFAT16	2193408	185472	90.6MB

	EnCase Report Case: DI-064 Page = = = = Measurement Logs = = = = Sectors Compared 3335472 Sectors Differ 5041 Diffs range 40494, 3330432-3335471 Hash computed for this case (DI-064) Hash after test: D0FC573FF774F6897BE520153C9BF770E998428F
Expected Results:	Source disk is unchanged src compares qualified equal to dst error message logged
Actual Results:	BIOS Anomaly
Analysis:	Expected results not achieved

Case DI-067 for EnCase 3.20

Case Summary:	Create an image from a BIOS-IDE source disk to a BIOS-IDE destination disk where the source disk is the same size as the destination Introduce a write error writing to the image.
Tester Name:	JRL
Test Date:	Tue Sep 10 17:55:42 2002
PC:	Beta3
Disks:	Source: DOS Drive 80 Physical Label A1 Destination: DOS Drive 81 Physical Label A4 Image media: DOS Drive 80 Physical Label DB A1 is a Quantum Sirooco1700A with 3335472 sectors A4 is a Quantum Sirooco1700A with 3335472 sectors DB is a Fujitsu MPE3064AT with 12672450 sectors CD-ROM with PartitionMagic Pro 6.0 and boot floppy with run scripts FS-TST Release 1.0 CD-ROM + Baddisk 3.2 + Badx13 3.2
Source disk setup:	Linux EXT2 & DOS Fat16 Disk: A1 Host: JudgeDee Operator: JRL OS: Windows/Me Options: Typical Date: Tue Oct 16 11:24:16 2001 cmd: Z:\ss\DISKWIPE.EXE A1 JudgeDee 80 A1 /src /new_log X:\pm\pqmagic /cmd=X:\pm\nex-src.txt Load Operating System to Source disk cmd: Z:\ss\DISKHASH.EXE A1 JudgeDee 80 /before /new_log Disk hash = D0FC573FF774F6897BE520153C9BF770E998428F
Destination Setup:	No destination setup required
Error Setup:	Z:\ss\baddisk 81 5 5 5 3 10 > a:\err-067.txt return code 00010 on command 00003 from disk 00081 at address 00005/00005/00003
Execute:	Z:\ss\DISKHASH.EXE DI-067 Beta3 80 /comment A1(JRL) /new_log /after
Log files loc:	test-archive/encase/encase-3.20/DI-067
Log File Highlights:	Image file acquired from DOS Restore environment Windows 98 EnCase report for case DI-067 is in NOLOG.txt Message displayed during DOS acquire: Error in <file name> cannot write to this file

Case DI-067 for EnCase 3.20	
	= = = = Measurement Logs = = = = No compare log found for DI-067 Hash computed for this case (DI-067) Hash after test: D0FC573FF774F6897BE520153C9BF770E998428F
Expected Results:	Source disk is unchanged error message logged
Actual Results:	No anomalies
Analysis:	Expected results achieved

Case DI-069 for EnCase 3.20	
Case Summary:	Create an image from a BIOS-IDE source disk to a BIOS-IDE destination disk where the source disk is the same size as the destination
Tester Name:	JRL
Test Date:	Sat May 25 10:46:53 2002
PC:	Beta7
Disks:	Source: DOS Drive 80 Physical Label A1 Destination: DOS Drive 81 Physical Label D7 Image media: DOS Drive 80 Physical Label D3 A1 is a Quantum Sirooco1700A with 3335472 sectors D7 is a Quantum Sirooco1700A with 3335472 sectors D3 is a Fujitsu MPE3064AT with 12672450 sectors CD-ROM with PartitionMagic Pro 6.0 and boot floppy with run scripts FS-TST Release 1.0 CD-ROM + Baddisk 3.2 + Badx13 3.2
Source disk setup:	Linux EXT2 & DOS Fat16 Disk: A1 Host: JudgeDee Operator: JRL OS: Windows/Me Options: Typical Date: Tue Oct 16 11:24:16 2001 cmd: Z:\ss\DISKWIPE.EXE A1 JudgeDee 80 A1 /src /new_log X:\pm\pqmagic /cmd=X:\pm\nex-src.txt Load Operating System to Source disk cmd: Z:\ss\DISKHASH.EXE A1 JudgeDee 80 /before /new_log Disk hash = D0FC573FF774F6897BE520153C9BF770E998428F
Destination Setup:	Z:\ss\DISKWIPE.EXE DI-069 Beta7 81 D7 /noask /dst /new_log /comment JRL No partition table defined
Error Setup:	none
Execute:	Z:\ss\DISKWIPE.EXE DI-069 Beta7 81 D7 /noask /dst /new_log /comment JRL Z:\ss\DISKCMP.EXE DI-069 Beta7 80 A1 81 D7 /new_log /comment JRL Z:\ss\DISKHASH.EXE DI-069 Beta7 80 /comment A1(JRL) /new_log /after
Log files loc:	test-archive/encase/encase-3.20/DI-069
Log File Highlights:	Image file acquired from DOS Restore environment Windows 98 EnCase report for case DI-069 is in a1-069.txt Evidence Number "1" Alias "1" File "D:\A1.e01" was acquired by jrl at 05/24/02 08:42:36AM. The computer system clock read: 05/24/02 08:42:36AM. Evidence acquired under DOS 7.10 using version 3.20. File Integrity: Completely Verified, 0 Errors. Verification Hash: 4385E645B15A9B9456C54CB4AE9640C8 Drive Geometry: Total Size 1.6GB (3,334,464 sectors) Cylinders: 827 Heads: 64 Sectors: 63

Case DI-069 for EnCase 3.20

Partitions:

Code	Type	Start Sector	Total Sectors	Size
06	BIGDOS	0	1229760	600.5MB
83	Linux EXT2	2721600	64512	31.5MB
82	Linux Swap	2923200	411264	200.8MB
83	Linux EXT2	1431360	205632	100.4MB
06	BIGDOS	1636992	145152	70.9MB
16	HiddenFAT16	2193408	185472	90.6MB

EnCase Report
Case: A1   Page

= = = = Measurement Logs = = = =
Sectors Compared 3335472
Sectors Differ 5040
Diffs range 3330432-3335471
Hash computed for this case (DI-069)
Hash after test: D0FC573FF774F6897BE520153C9BF770E998428F

Expected Results:	Source disk is unchanged src compares equal to dst
Actual Results:	BIOS Anomaly
Analysis:	Expected results not achieved

Case DI-070 for EnCase 3.20

Case Summary:	Create an image from a BIOS-IDE source disk to a BIOS-IDE destination disk where the source disk is larger than the destination
Tester Name:	JRL
Test Date:	Sat May 25 10:44:19 2002
PC:	Beta3
Disks:	Source: DOS Drive 80 Physical Label A1 Destination: DOS Drive 81 Physical Label B9 Image media: DOS Drive 80 Physical Label D3 A1 is a Quantum Sirooco1700A with 3335472 sectors B9 is a WDC AC21600H with 3173184 sectors D3 is a Fujitsu MPE3064AT with 12672450 sectors CD-ROM with PartitionMagic Pro 6.0 and boot floppy with run scripts FS-TST Release 1.0 CD-ROM + Baddisk 3.2 + Badx13 3.2
Source disk setup:	Linux EXT2 & DOS Fat16 Disk: A1 Host: JudgeDee Operator: JRL OS: Windows/Me Options: Typical Date: Tue Oct 16 11:24:16 2001 cmd: Z:\ss\DISKWIPE.EXE A1 JudgeDee 80 A1 /src /new_log X:\pm\pqmagic /cmd=X:\pm\nex-src.txt Load Operating System to Source disk cmd: Z:\ss\DISKHASH.EXE A1 JudgeDee 80 /before /new_log Disk hash = D0FC573FF774F6897BE520153C9BF770E998428F
Destination Setup:	Z:\ss\DISKWIPE.EXE DI-070 Beta3 81 B9 /noask /dst /new_log /comment JRL No partition table defined
Error Setup:	none
Execute:	Z:\ss\DISKWIPE.EXE DI-070 Beta3 81 B9 /noask /dst /new_log /comment JRL Z:\ss\DISKCMP.EXE DI-070 Beta7 80 A1 81 B9 /new_log /comment JRL
Log files loc:	test-archive/encase/encase-3.20/DI-070
Log File Highlights:	Image file acquired from DOS Restore environment Windows 98 EnCase report for case DI-070 is in a1-069.txt Evidence Number "1" Alias "1" File "D:\A1.e01" was acquired by jrl at 05/24/02 08:42:36AM. The computer system clock read: 05/24/02 08:42:36AM. Evidence acquired under DOS 7.10 using version 3.20.

```
File Integrity:
Completely Verified, 0 Errors.
Verification Hash:      4385E645B15A9B9456C54CB4AE9640C8

Drive Geometry:
Total Size      1.6GB (3,334,464 sectors)
Cylinders:      827
Heads: 64
Sectors:        63
```

Partitions:

Code	Type	Start Sector	Total Sectors	Size
06	BIGDOS	0	1229760	600.5MB
83	Linux EXT2	2721600	64512	31.5MB
82	Linux Swap	2923200	411264	200.8MB
83	Linux EXT2	1431360	205632	100.4MB
06	BIGDOS	1636992	145152	70.9MB
16	HiddenFAT16	2193408	185472	90.6MB

```
EnCase Report
Case: A1        Page

= = = = Measurement Logs = = = =
Sectors Compared 3173184
Sectors Differ 4032
Diffs range 3169152-3173183
Source (3335472) has 162288 more sectors than destination (3173184)
This case uses the hash computed from case DI-069
Hash after test: D0FC573FF774F6897BE520153C9BF770E998428F
```

Expected Results:	Source disk is unchanged src compares qualified equal to dst, src is truncated on dst truncation is logged
Actual Results:	BIOS Anomaly
Analysis:	Expected results not achieved

Case Summary:	Create an image from a BIOS-IDE source disk to a BIOS-IDE destination disk and the source contains a FAT16 partition where the source disk is smaller than the destination Introduce an error on the image.
Tester Name:	JRL
Test Date:	Thu Aug 29 15:32:46 2002
PC:	Beta3
Disks:	Source: DOS Drive 80 Physical Label A1 Destination: DOS Drive 81 Physical Label none Image media: DOS Drive 80 Physical Label D3 A1 is a Quantum Sirooco1700A with 3335472 sectors D3 is a Fujitsu MPE3064AT with 12672450 sectors CD-ROM with PartitionMagic Pro 6.0 and boot floppy with run scripts FS-TST Release 1.0 CD-ROM + Baddisk 3.2 + Badx13 3.2
Source disk setup:	Linux EXT2 & DOS Fat16 Disk: A1 Host: JudgeDee Operator: JRL OS: Windows/Me Options: Typical Date: Tue Oct 16 11:24:16 2001 cmd: Z:\ss\DISKWIPE.EXE A1 JudgeDee 80 A1 /src /new_log X:\pm\pqmagic /cmd=X:\pm\nex-src.txt Load Operating System to Source disk cmd: Z:\ss\DISKHASH.EXE A1 JudgeDee 80 /before /new_log

Case DI-071 for EnCase 3.20	
	Disk hash = D0FC573FF774F6897BE520153C9BF770E998428F
Destination Setup:	No destination setup required
Error Setup:	cmd: z:\ss\CORRUPT.EXE DI-071 Beta3 D:\a1-f16c.e01 8021043 39
	Comment: change 16/000/01 to 16/900/01 at LBA 16,128
Execute:	Z:\ss\DISKHASH.EXE DI-071 Beta7 80 /comment A1(JRL) /new_log /after
Log files loc:	test-archive/encase/encase-3.20/DI-071
Log File Highlights:	Image file acquired from DOS

Restore environment Windows 98
EnCase report for case DI-071 is in 071.txt
Evidence Number "a4" Alias "a4"

File "D:\A4-f16c.e01" was acquired by JRL at 08/29/02 01:34:57PM.
The computer system clock read: 08/29/02 01:34:57PM.

Evidence acquired under DOS 7.10 using version 3.20.

The integrity of the following sector groups could not be
verified:16064-16127
Drive Geometry:
Total Size   600.4MB (1,229,697 sectors)

Volume "a4" Parameters

File System:	FAT16	Drive Type:	Fixed
Sectors Per Cluster:	32	Bytes Per Sector:	512
Total Sectors:	1,229,697	Total Capacity:	629,424,128 bytes (600.3MB)
Total Clusters:	38,417	Unallocated:	625,491,968 bytes (596.5MB)
Free Clusters:	38,177	Allocated:	3,932,160 bytes (3.8MB)
Volume Name:		Volume Offset:	0
OEM Version:	MSWIN4.1	Volume Serial #:	3BCC-0C05
Heads:	64	Sectors Per Track:	63
Unused Sectors:	63	Number of FATs:	2
Sectors Per FAT:	151	Boot Sectors:	1

EnCase Report
Case: di-071c Page

= = = = Measurement Logs = = = =
No compare log found for DI-071
Hash computed for this case (DI-071)
Hash after test: D0FC573FF774F6897BE520153C9BF770E998428F

Expected Results:	Source disk is unchanged
	image verification error
Actual Results:	No anomalies
Analysis:	Expected results achieved

Case DI-072 for EnCase 3.20	
Case Summary:	Create an image from a BIOS-IDE source disk
	to a BIOS-IDE destination disk
	and the source contains a FAT32 partition
	where the source disk is smaller than the destination
Tester Name:	JRL
Test Date:	Tue Jun 11 17:11:53 2002
PC:	Beta7
Disks:	Source: DOS Drive 80 Physical Label F1
	Destination: DOS Drive 81 Physical Label A4
	Image media: DOS Drive 80 Physical Label D3

Case DI-072 for EnCase 3.20	
	F1 is a Quantum Sirooco1700A with 3335472 sectors
	A4 is a Quantum Sirooco1700A with 3335472 sectors
	D3 is a Fujitsu MPE3064AT with 12672450 sectors
	CD-ROM with PartitionMagic Pro 6.0 and boot floppy with run scripts
	FS-TST Release 1.0 CD-ROM + Baddisk 3.2 + Badx13 3.2
Source disk setup:	Linux EXT2 & Fat32
	Disk: F1
	Host: JudgeDee
	Operator: JRL
	OS: Windows/Me
	Options: Typical
	Date: Fri Nov 16 10:42:33 2001
	cmd: Z:\ss\DISKWIPE.EXE F1 JudgeDee 80 F1 /src /new_log
	X:\pm\pqmagic /cmd=X:\pm\f32-src.txt
	Load Operating System to Source disk
	cmd: Z:\ss\DISKHASH.EXE F1 JudgeDee 80 /before /new_log
	Disk hash = 3E7E5E0AB0FA333BE39D267F0DB8E340386DC05A
Destination Setup:	Z:\ss\DISKWIPE.EXE DI-072 Beta7 81 A4 /noask /dst /new_log /comment JRL
	See CMPPTLOG.TXT for partition table
Error Setup:	none
Execute:	Z:\ss\DISKWIPE.EXE DI-072 Beta7 81 A4 /noask /dst /new_log /comment JRL
	Z:\ss\PARTCMP.EXE DI-072 Beta7 80 F1 81 A4 /new_log /comment JRL
	/select 1 1
	Z:\ss\DISKHASH.EXE DI-072 Beta7 80 /comment F1(JRL) /new_log /after
Log files loc:	test-archive/encase/encase-3.20/DI-072
Log File Highlights:	Source disk Drive 0x80, BIOS: Legacy
	Interrupt 13 bios 0825/063/63 (max cyl/hd values)
	Interrupt 13 ext 00826/064/63 (number of cyl/hd)
	3330432 total number of sectors reported via interrupt 13 from the BIOS
	N Start LBA Length Start C/H/S End C/H/S boot Partition type
	1 P 000000063 001229697 0000/001/01 0304/063/63 Boot 0B Fat32
	2 X 001431360 001290240 0355/000/01 0674/063/63 05 extended
	3 S 000000063 000205569 0355/001/01 0405/063/63 83 Linux
	4 x 000205632 000145152 0406/000/01 0441/063/63 05 extended
	5 S 000000063 000145089 0406/001/01 0441/063/63 0B Fat32
	6 x 000762048 000185472 0544/000/01 0589/063/63 05 extended
	7 S 000000063 000185409 0544/001/01 0589/063/63 16 other
	8 S 000000000 000000000 0000/000/00 0000/000/00 00 empty entry
	9 P 002721600 000064512 0675/000/01 0690/063/63 83 Linux
	10 P 002923200 000411264 0725/000/01 0826/063/63 82 Linux swap
	Destination disk Drive 0x81, BIOS: Legacy
	Interrupt 13 bios 0825/063/63 (max cyl/hd values)
	Interrupt 13 ext 00826/064/63 (number of cyl/hd)
	3330432 total number of sectors reported via interrupt 13 from the BIOS
	N Start LBA Length Start C/H/S End C/H/S boot Partition type
	1 P 000000063 001334529 0000/001/01 0330/063/63 0B Fat32
	2 P 000000000 000000000 0000/000/00 0000/000/00 00 empty entry
	3 P 000000000 000000000 0000/000/00 0000/000/00 00 empty entry
	4 P 000000000 000000000 0000/000/00 0000/000/00 00 empty entry
	Image file acquired from DOS
	Restore environment Windows 98
	EnCase report for case DI-072 is in F1-F32.txt
	Evidence Number "1" Alias "1"
	File "E:\F1-f32.e01" was acquired by JRL at 06/11/02 05:07:34PM.
	The computer system clock read: 06/11/02 05:07:34PM.
	Evidence acquired under DOS 7.10 using version 3.20.
	File Integrity:
	Completely Verified, 0 Errors.
	Verification Hash: B3003D35A64A32963FFB8FB2EEA26581
	Drive Geometry:
	Total Size 600.4MB (1,229,697 sectors)

Volume "1" Parameters

File System:	FAT32	Drive Type:	Fixed
Sectors Per Cluster:	1	Bytes Per Sector:	512
Total Sectors:	1,229,697	Total Capacity:	619,901,440 bytes (591.2MB)
Total Clusters:	1,210,745	Unallocated:	97,435,136 bytes (92.9MB)
Free Clusters:	190,303	Allocated:	522,466,304 bytes (498.3MB)
Volume Name:		Volume Offset:	0
OEM Version:	MSWIN4.1	Volume Serial #:	0000-0000
Heads:	64	Sectors Per Track:	63
Unused Sectors:	63	Number of FATs:	2
Sectors Per FAT:	9,460	Boot Sectors:	32

```
EnCase Report
Case: F1-F32    Page

= = = = Measurement Logs = = = =
Sectors Compared 1229697
Sectors Differ 1
Diffs range:  1
Source (1229697) has 104832 fewer sectors than destination (1334529)
Zero fill:      0
Src Byte fill (F1): 0
Dst Byte fill (A4): 104832
Other fill:     0
Other no fill: 0
Hash computed for this case (DI-072)
Hash after test: 3E7E5E0AB0FA333BE39D267F0DB8E340386DC05A
```

Expected Results:	Source disk is unchanged src compares qualified equal to dst
Actual Results:	Logical restore anomaly
Analysis:	Expected results not achieved

Case Summary:	Create an image from a BIOS-IDE source disk to a BIOS-IDE destination disk and the source contains a FAT16 partition where the source disk is the same size as the destination Introduce a write error writing to the image.
Tester Name:	JRL
Test Date:	Tue Sep 10 17:00:38 2002
PC:	Beta3
Disks:	Source: DOS Drive 80 Physical Label A1 Destination: DOS Drive 81 Physical Label A4 Image media: DOS Drive 80 Physical Label DB A1 is a Quantum Sirooco1700A with 3335472 sectors A4 is a Quantum Sirooco1700A with 3335472 sectors DB is a Fujitsu MPE3064AT with 12672450 sectors CD-ROM with PartitionMagic Pro 6.0 and boot floppy with run scripts FS-TST Release 1.0 CD-ROM + Baddisk 3.2 + Badx13 3.2
Source disk setup:	Linux EXT2 & DOS Fat16 Disk: A1 Host: JudgeDee Operator: JRL OS: Windows/Me Options: Typical Date: Tue Oct 16 11:24:16 2001 cmd: Z:\ss\DISKWIPE.EXE A1 JudgeDee 80 A1 /src /new_log X:\pm\pqmagic /cmd=X:\pm\nex-src.txt Load Operating System to Source disk

Case DI-082 for EnCase 3.20

	cmd: Z:\ss\DISKHASH.EXE A1 JudgeDee 80 /before /new_log Disk hash = D0FC573FF774F6897BE520153C9BF770E998428F
Destination Setup:	No destination setup required
Error Setup:	Z:\ss\baddisk 81 2 2 8 3 10 > a:\err-082.txt return code 00010 on command 00003 from disk 00081 at address 00002/00002/00008
Execute:	
Log files loc:	test-archive/encase/encase-3.20/DI-082
Log File Highlights:	Image file acquired from DOS Restore environment Windows 98 EnCase report for case DI-082 is in NOLOG.txt Message displayed during DOS acquire: Error in <file name> cannot write to this file = = = = Measurement Logs = = = = No compare log found for DI-082 This case uses the hash computed from case DI-067 Hash after test: D0FC573FF774F6897BE520153C9BF770E998428F
Expected Results:	Source disk is unchanged error message logged
Actual Results:	No anomalies
Analysis:	Expected results achieved

Case DI-083 for EnCase 3.20

Case Summary:	Create an image from a BIOS-IDE source disk to a BIOS-IDE destination disk and the source contains a FAT32 partition where the source disk is the same size as the destination Introduce an error on the image.
Tester Name:	JRL
Test Date:	Thu Aug 29 14:33:11 2002
PC:	Beta3
Disks:	Source: DOS Drive 80 Physical Label F1 Destination: DOS Drive 81 Physical Label none Image media: DOS Drive 80 Physical Label D3 F1 is a Quantum Sirooco1700A with 3335472 sectors D3 is a Fujitsu MPE3064AT with 12672450 sectors CD-ROM with PartitionMagic Pro 6.0 and boot floppy with run scripts FS-TST Release 1.0 CD-ROM + Baddisk 3.2 + Badx13 3.2
Source disk setup:	Linux EXT2 & Fat32 Disk: F1 Host: JudgeDee Operator: JRL OS: Windows/Me Options: Typical Date: Fri Nov 16 10:42:33 2001 cmd: Z:\ss\DISKWIPE.EXE F1 JudgeDee 80 F1 /src /new_log X:\pm\pqmagic /cmd=X:\pm\f32-src.txt Load Operating System to Source disk cmd: Z:\ss\DISKHASH.EXE F1 JudgeDee 80 /before /new_log Disk hash = 3E7E5E0AB0FA333BE39D267F0DB8E340386DC05A
Destination Setup:	No destination setup required
Error Setup:	cmd: z:\ss\CORRUPT.EXE DI-083 Beta3 D:\f1-f32c.e01 475977010 38 Comment: change 00922/010/10 to 00920/810/10 (930015)
Execute:	Z:\ss\DISKHASH.EXE DI-083 JudgeDee 80 /comment F1(JRL) /new_log /after
Log files loc:	test-archive/encase/encase-3.20/DI-083
Log File Highlights:	Image file acquired from DOS Restore environment Windows 98 EnCase report for case DI-083 is in 083.txt Evidence Number "F1-F32" Alias "F1-F32" File "D:\F1-f32c.e01" was acquired by JRL at 08/29/02 02:35:54PM. The computer system clock read: 08/29/02 02:35:54PM. Evidence acquired under DOS 7.10 using version 3.20. The integrity of the following sector groups could not be

Case DI-083 for EnCase 3.20

verified:929920-929983
Drive Geometry:
Total Size   600.4MB (1,229,697 sectors)

Volume "F1-F32" Parameters

File System:	FAT32	Drive Type:	Fixed
Sectors Per Cluster:	1	Bytes Per Sector:	512
Total Sectors:	1,229,697	Total Capacity:	619,901,440 bytes (591.2MB)
Total Clusters:	1,210,745	Unallocated:	97,435,136 bytes (92.9MB)
Free Clusters:	190,303	Allocated:	522,466,304 bytes (498.3MB)
Volume Name:		Volume Offset:	0
OEM Version:	MSWIN4.1	Volume Serial #:	0000-0000
Heads:	64	Sectors Per Track:	63
Unused Sectors:	63	Number of FATs:	2
Sectors Per FAT:	9,460	Boot Sectors:	32

EnCase Report
Case: f1-f32   Page

= = = = Measurement Logs = = = =
No compare log found for DI-083
Hash computed for this case (DI-083)
Hash after test: 3E7E5E0AB0FA333BE39D267F0DB8E340386DC05A

Expected Results:	Source disk is unchanged image verification error
Actual Results:	No anomalies
Analysis:	Expected results achieved

Case DI-084 for EnCase 3.20

Case Summary:	Create an image from a BIOS-IDE source disk to a BIOS-IDE destination disk and the source contains a NTFS partition where the source disk is the same size as the destination
Tester Name:	JRL
Test Date:	Mon Nov 11 22:59:33 2002
PC:	McCloud
Disks:	Source: DOS Drive 80 Physical Label F6 Destination: DOS Drive 81 Physical Label 64 Image media: DOS Drive 80 Physical Label 75 F6 is an IBM-DTLA-307020 with 40188960 sectors 64 is a WDCWD64AA with 12594960 sectors 75 is a IC35L040AVER07-0 with 80418240 sectors CD-ROM with PartitionMagic Pro 6.0 and boot floppy with run scripts FS-TST Release 1.0 CD-ROM + Baddisk 3.2 + Badx13 3.2
Source disk setup:	Windows 2000 with NTFS & Fat32 Disk: F6 Host: Wimsey Operator: JRL OS: Windows 2000 Date: Sat Jul 21 15:53:12 2001 DISKWIPE.EXE F6_SRC Wimsey 80 F6 /src /new_log /noask /comment Windows 2000/NT source X:\pm\pqmagic /cmd=X:\pm\nt-src.txt Load Operating System to Source disk DISKHASH.EXE LX-27 Morse 80 /before Disk hash = 8034683D5D55BA51409AC7B5CB0845CA2CF6B235

Case DI-084 for EnCase 3.20

Destination Setup:	Z:\ss\DISKWIPE.EXE DI-084 McCloud 81 64 /noask /dst /new_log /comment JRL See CMPPTLOG.TXT for partition table
Error Setup:	none
Execute:	Z:\ss\DISKWIPE.EXE DI-084 McCloud 81 64 /noask /dst /new_log /comment JRL Z:\ss\PARTCMP.EXE DI-084 Rumpole 80 F6 81 64 /new_log /comment JRL /select 5 1 Z:\ss\DISKHASH.EXE DI-084 Wimsey 80 /comment F6(JRL) /new_log /after
Log files loc:	test-archive/encase/encase-3.20/DI-084
Log File Highlights:	Source disk Drive 0x80, BIOS: Extensions Present Interrupt 13 bios 1023/254/63 (max cyl/hd values) Interrupt 13 ext 16383/016/63 (number of cyl/hd) 40188960 total number of sectors reported via interrupt 13 from the BIOS

```
 N   Start LBA Length    Start C/H/S   End C/H/S    boot Partition type
 1 P 000000063 006152832 0000/001/01 0382/254/63 Boot 0B Fat32
 2 X 008193150 031985415 0510/000/01 1023/254/63      0F extended
 3 S 000000000 000000000 0000/000/00 0000/000/00      00 empty entry
 4 x 002056320 001237005 0638/000/01 0714/254/63      05 extended
 5 S 000000063 001236942 0638/001/01 0714/254/63      07 NTFS
 6 x 005349645 001638630 0843/000/01 0944/254/63      05 extended
 7 S 000000063 001638567 0843/001/01 0944/254/63      17 other
 8 x 030748410 001237005 1023/000/01 1023/254/63      05 extended
 9 S 000000063 001236942 1023/001/01 1023/254/63      1B other
10 S 000000000 000000000 0000/000/00 0000/000/00      00 empty entry
11 P 000000000 000000000 0000/000/00 0000/000/00      00 empty entry
12 P 000000000 000000000 0000/000/00 0000/000/00      00 empty entry
```

Destination disk Drive 0x81, BIOS: Extensions Present
Interrupt 13 bios 0783/254/63 (max cyl/hd values)
Interrupt 13 ext 13328/015/63 (number of cyl/hd)
12594960 total number of sectors reported via interrupt 13 from the BIOS

```
 N   Start LBA Length    Start C/H/S   End C/H/S    boot Partition type
 1 P 000000063 001236942 0000/001/01 0076/254/63      07 NTFS
 2 P 000000000 000000000 0000/000/00 0000/000/00      00 empty entry
 3 P 000000000 000000000 0000/000/00 0000/000/00      00 empty entry
 4 P 000000000 000000000 0000/000/00 0000/000/00      00 empty entry
```

Image file acquired from FastBloc
Restore environment Windows 2000
EnCase report for case DI-084 is in 084.txt
Evidence Number "F6-NT"   Alias "F6-NT"

File "D:\F6-NT.E01" was acquired by JRL at 11/11/02 11:21:00PM.
The computer system clock read: 11/11/02 11:21:33PM.

Evidence acquired under Windows 2000 using version 3.20.

File Integrity:
Completely Verified, 0 Errors.
Acquisition Hash: 2E0E8B17165DB4BC9FE1FADDD3F10E3F
Verification Hash: 2E0E8B17165DB4BC9FE1FADDD3F10E3F

Drive Geometry:
Total Size   604.0MB (1,236,940 sectors)

Volume "F6-NT" Parameters

File System:	NTFS	Drive Type:	Fixed
Sectors Per Cluster:	2	Bytes Per Sector:	512
Total Sectors:	1,236,940	Total Capacity:	633,313,280 bytes (604.0MB)
Total Clusters:	618,470	Unallocated:	628,548,608 bytes (599.4MB)
Free Clusters:	613,817	Allocated:	4,764,672 bytes (4.5MB)
Volume Name:		Volume Offset:	0

Case DI-084 for EnCase 3.20

	EnCase Report Case: DI-084　Page = = = = Measurement Logs = = = = Sectors Compared 1236942 Sectors Differ 2 Diffs range:　1236940-1236941 Hash computed for this case (DI-084) Hash after test: 8034683D5D55BA51409AC7B5CB0845CA2CF6B235
Expected Results:	Source disk is unchanged src compares equal to dst
Actual Results:	No anomalies
Analysis:	Expected results achieved

Case DI-089 for EnCase 3.20

Case Summary:	Create an image from a BIOS-IDE source disk to a BIOS-IDE destination disk and the source contains a FAT32 partition where the source disk is larger than the destination
Tester Name:	JRL
Test Date:	Tue Oct 22 08:08:25 2002
PC:	Beta3
Disks:	Source: DOS Drive 80 Physical Label 60 Destination: DOS Drive 81 Physical Label 61 Image media: DOS Drive 80 Physical Label DB 60 is a WDCWD64AA with 12594960 sectors 61 is a WDCWD64AA with 12594960 sectors DB is a Fujitsu MPE3064AT with 12672450 sectors CD-ROM with PartitionMagic Pro 6.0 and boot floppy with run scripts FS-TST Release 1.0 CD-ROM + Baddisk 3.2 + Badx13 3.2
Source disk setup:	Linux EXT2 & Fat32 Disk: 60 Host: JudgeDee Operator: JRL OS: No_os Options: none Date: Fri Oct 18 10:53:57 2002 cmd: Z:\ss\DISKWIPE.EXE 60 JudgeDee 80 60 /src /new_log X:\pm\pqmagic /cmd=X:\pm\f32-src.txt Load Operating System to Source disk cmd: z:\ss\DISKHASH.EXE 60 JudgeDee 80 /before /new_log Disk hash　= B54E43E5B3422D7519ABEA166841DD3FC6CC2015
Destination Setup:	Z:\ss\DISKWIPE.EXE DI-089 Beta3 81 61 /noask /dst /new_log /comment JRL See CMPPTLOG.TXT for partition table
Error Setup:	none
Execute:	Z:\ss\DISKWIPE.EXE DI-089 Beta3 81 61 /noask /dst /new_log /comment JRL Z:\ss\PARTCMP.EXE DI-089 Beta3 80 60 81 61 /new_log /comment JRL /select 1 1 Z:\ss\DISKHASH.EXE DI-089 Beta3 80 /comment 60(JRL) /new_log /after
Log files loc:	test-archive/encase/encase-3.20/DI-089
Log File Highlights:	Source disk Drive 0x80, BIOS: Legacy Interrupt 13　bios　0782/254/63 (max cyl/hd values) Interrupt 13　ext　00783/255/63 (number of cyl/hd) 12578895 total number of sectors reported via interrupt 13 from the BIOS 　N　　Start LBA Length　　Start C/H/S End C/H/S　boot Partition type 　1 P 000000063 001236942 0000/001/01 0076/254/63 Boot 0B Fat32 　2 X 001429785 010554705 0089/000/01 0745/254/63　　　05 extended 　3 S 000000063 000208782 0089/001/01 0101/254/63　　　83 Linux 　4 x 000208845 000144585 0102/000/01 0110/254/63　　　05 extended 　5 S 000000063 000144522 0102/001/01 0110/254/63　　　0B Fat32 　6 x 000771120 000192780 0137/000/01 0148/254/63　　　05 extended 　7 S 000000063 000192717 0137/001/01 0148/254/63　　　16 other 　8 S 000000000 000000000 0000/000/00 0000/000/00　　　00 empty entry 　9 P 011984490 000064260 0746/000/01 0749/254/63　　　83 Linux 10 P 012177270 000417690 0758/000/01 0783/254/63　　　82 Linux swap Destination disk Drive 0x81, BIOS: Legacy Interrupt 13　bios　0782/254/63 (max cyl/hd values) Interrupt 13　ext　00783/255/63 (number of cyl/hd)

12578895 total number of sectors reported via interrupt 13 from the BIOS

```
 N   Start LBA Length      Start C/H/S End C/H/S   boot Partition type
 1 P 000000063 001140552 0000/001/01 0070/254/63      0B Fat32
 2 P 000000000 000000000 0000/000/00 0000/000/00      00 empty entry
 3 P 000000000 000000000 0000/000/00 0000/000/00      00 empty entry
 4 P 000000000 000000000 0000/000/00 0000/000/00      00 empty entry
```

Image file acquired from DOS
Restore environment Windows 2000
EnCase report for case DI-089 is in DI-089.txt
Evidence Number "60-F32"   Alias "60-F32"

File "D:\60-F32.E01" was acquired by JRL at 10/22/02 08:43:18AM.
The computer system clock read: 10/22/02 08:43:18AM.

Evidence acquired under DOS 7.10 using version 3.20.

File Integrity:
Completely Verified, 0 Errors.
Verification Hash: D469C8468A9DAEA4BB72A062A366D418

Drive Geometry:
Total Size   604.0MB (1,236,942 sectors)

Volume "60-F32" Parameters

File System:	FAT32	Drive Type:	Fixed
Sectors Per Cluster:	1	Bytes Per Sector:	512
Total Sectors:	1,236,942	Total Capacity:	623,553,536 bytes (594.7MB)
Total Clusters:	1,217,878	Unallocated:	623,550,464 bytes (594.7MB)
Free Clusters:	1,217,872	Allocated:	3,072 bytes (3.0KB)
Volume Name:		Volume Offset:	0
OEM Version:	MSWIN4.1	Volume Serial #:	0000-0000
Heads:	255	Sectors Per Track:	63
Unused Sectors:	63	Number of FATs:	2
Sectors Per FAT:	9,516	Boot Sectors:	32

EnCase Report
Case: DI-89   Page

= = = = Measurement Logs = = = =
Sectors Compared 1140552
Sectors Differ 3
Diffs range: 1, 32, 9548
Source (1236942) has 96390 more sectors than destination (1140552)
Hash computed for this case (DI-089)
Hash after test: B54E43E5B3422D7519ABEA166841DD3FC6CC2015

Expected Results:	Source disk is unchanged src compares qualified equal to dst, src is truncated on dst truncation is logged
Actual Results:	Logical restore anomaly
Analysis:	Expected results not achieved

Case DI-091 for EnCase 3.20	
Case Summary:	Create an image from an XBIOS-IDE source disk to an XBIOS-IDE destination disk where the source disk is smaller than the destination Introduce an error on the image.
Tester Name:	JRL
Test Date:	Fri Aug 30 05:46:08 2002
PC:	HecRamsey

Case DI-091 for EnCase 3.20	
Disks:	Source: DOS Drive 80 Physical Label A5 Destination: DOS Drive 81 Physical Label none Image media: DOS Drive 80 Physical Label 7C A5 is a WDC WD200BB-00AUA1 with 39102336 sectors 7C is a MAXTOR 6L040J2 with 78177792 sectors CD-ROM with PartitionMagic Pro 6.0 and boot floppy with run scripts FS-TST Release 1.0 CD-ROM + Baddisk 3.2 + Badx13 3.2
Source disk setup:	Fat32 only Disk: A5 Host: JudgeDee Operator: JRL OS: NoOs Options: none Date: Mon Apr 15 14:35:04 2002 cmd: Z:\ss\DISKWIPE.EXE A5 JudgeDee 80 A5 /src /new_log X:\pm\pqmagic /cmd=X:\pm\f32-src.txt No OS loaded, FAT32 partition only cmd: Z:\ss\DISKHASH.EXE A5 JudgeDee 80 /before /new_log Disk hash = 3DE5C01B5BB337EA3E6CF9BC25EB844F5D00FD14
Destination Setup:	No destination setup required
Error Setup:	cmd: Z:\ss\CORRUPT.EXE DI-091 HecRamsey D:\A5.e09 78544 39 Comment: Change 32498/009/01 to 32498/099/01 at LBA 32758551???
Execute:	Z:\ss\DISKHASH.EXE DI-091 HecRamsey 80 /comment A5(JRL) /new_log /after
Log files loc:	test-archive/encase/encase-3.20/DI-091
Log File Highlights:	Image file acquired from DOS Restore environment Windows 2000 EnCase report for case DI-091 is in 091.txt Evidence Number "A5" Alias "A5" File "F:\A5.E01" was acquired by JRL at 08/30/02 05:51:57AM. The computer system clock read: 08/30/02 05:51:57AM. Evidence acquired under DOS 7.10 using version 3.20. The integrity of the following sector groups could not be verified:32758528-32758591 Drive Geometry: Total Size 18.6GB (39,102,336 sectors) Cylinders: 16,383 Heads: 16 Sectors: 63

Partitions:

Code	Type	Start Sector	Total Sectors	Size
0B	FAT32	0	1237005	604.0MB
83	Linux EXT2	38491740	64260	31.4MB
82	Linux Swap	38684520	417690	204.0MB
83	Linux EXT2	1429785	208845	102.0MB
0B	FAT32	1638630	144585	70.6MB
16	HiddenFAT16	2200905	192780	94.1MB

EnCase Report
Case: DI-091   Page

= = = = Measurement Logs = = = =
No compare log found for DI-091
Hash computed for this case (DI-091)
Hash after test: 3DE5C01B5BB337EA3E6CF9BC25EB844F5D00FD14

Expected Results:	Source disk is unchanged image verification error
Actual Results:	No anomalies
Analysis:	Expected results achieved

Case DI-092 for EnCase 3.20	
Case Summary:	Create an image from an XBIOS-IDE source disk to an XBIOS-IDE destination disk where the source disk is smaller than the destination
Tester Name:	JRL
Test Date:	Fri May 24 16:36:04 2002
PC:	Cadfael
Disks:	Source: DOS Drive 80 Physical Label F5 Destination: DOS Drive 81 Physical Label 7B Image media: DOS Drive 80 Physical Label 70 F5 is an IBM-DTLA-307020 with 40188960 sectors 7B is a MAXTOR 6L040J2 with 78177792 sectors 70 is a IC35L040AVER07-0 with 80418240 sectors CD-ROM with PartitionMagic Pro 6.0 and boot floppy with run scripts FS-TST Release 1.0 CD-ROM + Baddisk 3.2 + Badx13 3.2
Source disk setup:	Dual boot Linux/Windows Me with EXT2 & Fat16 Disk: F5 Host: Cadfael Operator: JRL OS: WindowsMe/Linux Date: Sat Aug 11 11:13:43 2001 DISKWIPE.EXE F5_SRC Cadfael 80 F5 /src X:\pm\pqmagic /cmd=X:\pm\fat-src.txt Load Operating System to Source disk DISKHASH.EXE F5_SRC Cadfael 80 /before Disk hash = 83A0002816BBF089F8BE33C41C92C3B5A0F42A54
Destination Setup:	Z:\ss\DISKWIPE.EXE DI-092 Cadfael 81 7B /noask /dst /new_log /comment JRL No partition table defined
Error Setup:	none
Execute:	Z:\ss\DISKWIPE.EXE DI-092 Cadfael 81 7B /noask /dst /new_log /comment JRL Z:\ss\DISKCMP.EXE DI-092 Rumpole 80 F5 81 7B /new_log /comment JRL
Log files loc:	test-archive/encase/encase-3.20/DI-092
Log File Highlights:	Image file acquired from DOS Restore environment Windows 2000 EnCase report for case DI-092 is in F5.txt Evidence Number "F5" Alias "F5" File "D:\F5.E01" was acquired by JRL at 05/24/02 05:11:33PM. The computer system clock read: 05/24/02 05:11:33PM. Evidence acquired under DOS 7.10 using version 3.20. Acquisition Notes: none. File Integrity: Completely Verified, 0 Errors. Verification Hash: 849BAEFDE9407109B9D22FBB479FE00D Drive Geometry: Total Size 19.2GB (40,188,960 sectors) Cylinders: 16,383 Heads: 16 Sectors: 63

Partitions:

Code	Type	Start Sector	Total Sectors	Size
06	BIGDOS	0	1237005	604.0MB
83	Linux EXT2	9430155	6152895	2.9GB
82	Linux Swap	39760875	417690	204.0MB
83	Linux EXT2	2249100	208845	102.0MB
06	BIGDOS	2457945	144585	70.6MB
16	HiddenFAT16	6699105	192780	94.1MB

Case DI-092 for EnCase 3.20	
	EnCase Report Case: F5 Page = = = = Measurement Logs = = = = Sectors Compared 40188960 Sectors Differ 0 Diffs range Source (40188960) has 37988832 fewer sectors than destination (78177792) Zero fill: 0 Src Byte fill (F5): 0 Dst Byte fill (7B): 37988832 Other fill: 0 Other no fill: 0 This case uses the hash computed from case DI-098 Hash after test: 83A0002816BBF089F8BE33C41C92C3B5A0F42A54
Expected Results:	Source disk is unchanged src compares qualified equal to dst
Actual Results:	No anomalies
Analysis:	Expected results achieved

Case DI-093 for EnCase 3.20	
Case Summary:	Create an image from an XBIOS-IDE source disk to an XBIOS-IDE destination disk where the source disk is the same size as the destination Introduce a read error from the source.
Tester Name:	JRL
Test Date:	Fri Oct 18 08:51:10 2002
PC:	HecRamsey
Disks:	Source: DOS Drive 80 Physical Label F5 Destination: DOS Drive 81 Physical Label F8 Image media: DOS Drive 80 Physical Label 7C F5 is an IBM-DTLA-307020 with 40188960 sectors F8 is an IBM-DTLA-307020 with 40188960 sectors 7C is a MAXTOR 6L040J2 with 78177792 sectors CD-ROM with PartitionMagic Pro 6.0 and boot floppy with run scripts FS-TST Release 1.0 CD-ROM + Baddisk 3.2 + Badx13 3.2
Source disk setup:	Dual boot Linux/Windows Me with EXT2 & Fat16 Disk: F5 Host: Cadfael Operator: JRL OS: WindowsMe/Linux Date: Sat Aug 11 11:13:43 2001 DISKWIPE.EXE F5_SRC Cadfael 80 F5 /src X:\pm\pqmagic /cmd=X:\pm\fat-src.txt Load Operating System to Source disk DISKHASH.EXE F5_SRC Cadfael 80 /before Disk hash = 83A0002816BBF089F8BE33C41C92C3B5A0F42A54
Destination Setup:	Z:\ss\DISKWIPE.EXE DI-093 HecRamsey 81 F8 /noask /dst /new_log /comment JRL No partition table defined
Error Setup:	Z:\ss\badx13 81 42 10 1357 > a:\err-093.txt Return error code 10 for X13 command 42 from drive 81 at LBA sector 1,357
Execute:	Z:\ss\DISKWIPE.EXE DI-093 HecRamsey 81 F8 /noask /dst /new_log /comment JRL Z:\ss\DISKCMP.EXE DI-093 HecRamsey 80 F5 81 F8 /new_log /comment JRL Z:\ss\DISKHASH.EXE DI-093 Wimsey 80 /comment F5(JRL) /new_log /after
Log files loc:	test-archive/encase/encase-3.20/DI-093
Log File Highlights:	Image file acquired from DOS Restore environment Windows 2000 EnCase report for case DI-093 is in 093.txt Evidence Number "F5-rd-err" Alias "F5-rd-err" File "D:\F5-ERR.E01" was acquired by JRL at 10/18/02 09:18:14AM. The computer system clock read: 10/18/02 09:18:14AM. Evidence acquired under DOS 7.10 using version 3.20. File Integrity:

Case DI-093 for EnCase 3.20

Completely Verified, 0 Errors.
Verification Hash: D527DD605E991E5767A4C1AC93E3B72F

The following sector blocks reported read errors during acquisition:
1344-1407

Drive Geometry:
Total Size   19.2GB (40,188,960 sectors)
Cylinders: 16,383
Heads: 16
Sectors: 63

Partitions:

Code	Type	Start Sector	Total Sectors	Size
06	BIGDOS	0	1237005	604.0MB
83	Linux EXT2	9430155	6152895	2.9GB
82	Linux Swap	39760875	417690	204.0MB
83	Linux EXT2	2249100	208845	102.0MB
06	BIGDOS	2457945	144585	70.6MB
16	HiddenFAT16	6699105	192780	94.1MB

EnCase Report
Case: DI-093   Page

= = = = Measurement Logs = = = =
Sectors Compared 40188960
Sectors Differ 10446
Diffs range 1357-1407, 40178565-40188959
Hash computed for this case (DI-093)
Hash after test: 83A0002816BBF089F8BE33C41C92C3B5A0F42A54

Expected Results:	Source disk is unchanged src compares qualified equal to dst error message logged
Actual Results:	Restore anomaly
Analysis:	Expected results not achieved

Case DI-098 for EnCase 3.20

Case Summary:	Create an image from an XBIOS-IDE source disk to an XBIOS-IDE destination disk where the source disk is the same size as the destination
Tester Name:	JRL
Test Date:	Fri May 24 15:33:02 2002
PC:	Rumpole
Disks:	Source: DOS Drive 80 Physical Label F5 Destination: DOS Drive 81 Physical Label F7 Image media: DOS Drive 80 Physical Label 70 F5 is an IBM-DTLA-307020 with 40188960 sectors F7 is an IBM-DTLA-307020 with 40188960 sectors 70 is a IC35L040AVER07-0 with 80418240 sectors CD-ROM with PartitionMagic Pro 6.0 and boot floppy with run scripts FS-TST Release 1.0 CD-ROM + Baddisk 3.2 + Badx13 3.2
Source disk setup:	Dual boot Linux/Windows Me with EXT2 & Fat16 Disk: F5 Host: Cadfael Operator: JRL OS: WindowsMe/Linux Date: Sat Aug 11 11:13:43 2001 DISKWIPE.EXE F5_SRC Cadfael 80 F5 /src X:\pm\pqmagic /cmd=X:\pm\fat-src.txt Load Operating System to Source disk DISKHASH.EXE F5_SRC Cadfael 80 /before Disk hash = 83A0002816BBF089F8BE33C41C92C3B5A0F42A54
Destination Setup:	Z:\ss\DISKWIPE.EXE DI-098 Rumpole 81 F7 /noask /dst /new_log /comment JRL

Case DI-098 for EnCase 3.20	
	No partition table defined
Error Setup:	none
Execute:	Z:\ss\DISKWIPE.EXE DI-098 Rumpole 81 F7 /noask /dst /new_log /comment JRL Z:\ss\DISKCMP.EXE DI-098 Rumpole 80 F5 81 F7 /new_log /comment JRL Z:\ss\DISKHASH.EXE DI-098 Rumpole 80 /comment F5(JRL) /new_log /after
Log files loc:	test-archive/encase/encase-3.20/DI-098
Log File Highlights:	Image file acquired from DOS Restore environment Windows 2000 EnCase report for case DI-098 is in F5.txt Evidence Number "F5" Alias "F5" File "D:\F5.E01" was acquired by JRL at 05/24/02 05:11:33PM. The computer system clock read: 05/24/02 05:11:33PM. Evidence acquired under DOS 7.10 using version 3.20. Acquisition Notes: none. File Integrity: Completely Verified, 0 Errors. Verification Hash: 849BAEFDE9407109B9D22FBB479FE00D Drive Geometry: Total Size 19.2GB (40,188,960 sectors) Cylinders: 16,383 Heads: 16 Sectors: 63 Partitions: | Code	Type	Start Sector	Total Sectors	Size
---	---	---	---	---
06	BIGDOS	0	1237005	604.0MB
83	Linux EXT2	9430155	6152895	2.9GB
82	Linux Swap	39760875	417690	204.0MB
83	Linux EXT2	2249100	208845	102.0MB
06	BIGDOS	2457945	144585	70.6MB
16	HiddenFAT16	6699105	192780	94.1MB	 EnCase Report Case: F5 Page = = = = Measurement Logs = = = = Sectors Compared 40188960 Sectors Differ 10395 Diffs range 40178565-40188959 Hash computed for this case (DI-098) Hash after test: 83A0002816BBF089F8BE33C41C92C3B5A0F42A54
Expected Results:	Source disk is unchanged src compares equal to dst
Actual Results:	Restore anomaly
Analysis:	Expected results not achieved

Case DI-099 for EnCase 3.20	
Case Summary:	Create an image from an XBIOS-IDE source disk to an XBIOS-IDE destination disk where the source disk is larger than the destination
Tester Name:	JRL
Test Date:	Fri May 24 16:32:36 2002
PC:	Wimsey
Disks:	Source: DOS Drive 80 Physical Label F5 Destination: DOS Drive 81 Physical Label A6 Image media: DOS Drive 80 Physical Label 70 F5 is an IBM-DTLA-307020 with 40188960 sectors A6 is a WDC WD200BB-00AUA1 with 39102336 sectors 70 is a IC35L040AVER07-0 with 80418240 sectors

Case DI-099 for EnCase 3.20	
	CD-ROM with PartitionMagic Pro 6.0 and boot floppy with run scripts
	FS-TST Release 1.0 CD-ROM + Baddisk 3.2 + Badx13 3.2
Source disk setup:	Dual boot Linux/Windows Me with EXT2 & Fat16
	Disk: F5
	Host: Cadfael
	Operator: JRL
	OS: WindowsMe/Linux
	Date: Sat Aug 11 11:13:43 2001
	DISKWIPE.EXE F5_SRC Cadfael 80 F5 /src
	X:\pm\pqmagic /cmd=X:\pm\fat-src.txt
	Load Operating System to Source disk
	DISKHASH.EXE F5_SRC Cadfael 80 /before
	Disk hash = 83A0002816BBF089F8BE33C41C92C3B5A0F42A54
Destination Setup:	Z:\ss\DISKWIPE.EXE DI-099 Wimsey 81 A6 /noask /dst /new_log /comment JRL
	No partition table defined
Error Setup:	none
Execute:	Z:\ss\DISKWIPE.EXE DI-099 Wimsey 81 A6 /noask /dst /new_log /comment JRL
	Z:\ss\DISKCMP.EXE DI-099 Rumpole 80 F5 81 A6 /new_log /comment JRL
Log files loc:	test-archive/encase/encase-3.20/DI-099
Log File Highlights:	Image file acquired from DOS
	Restore environment Windows 2000
	EnCase report for case DI-099 is in F5.txt
	Evidence Number "F5" Alias "F5"
	File "D:\F5.E01" was acquired by JRL at 05/24/02 05:11:33PM.
	The computer system clock read: 05/24/02 05:11:33PM.
	Evidence acquired under DOS 7.10 using version 3.20.
	Acquisition Notes:
	none.
	File Integrity:
	Completely Verified, 0 Errors.
	Verification Hash: 849BAEFDE9407109B9D22FBB479FE00D
	Drive Geometry:
	Total Size 19.2GB (40,188,960 sectors)
	Cylinders: 16,383
	Heads: 16
	Sectors: 63
	Partitions:

Code	Type	Start Sector	Total Sectors	Size
06	BIGDOS	0	1237005	604.0MB
83	Linux EXT2	9430155	6152895	2.9GB
82	Linux Swap	39760875	417690	204.0MB
83	Linux EXT2	2249100	208845	102.0MB
06	BIGDOS	2457945	144585	70.6MB
16	HiddenFAT16	6699105	192780	94.1MB

	EnCase Report
	Case: F5 Page
	= = = = Measurement Logs = = = =
	Sectors Compared 39102336
	Sectors Differ 126
	Diffs range 39102210-39102335
	Source (40188960) has 1086624 more sectors than destination (39102336)
	This case uses the hash computed from case DI-098
	Hash after test: 83A0002816BBF089F8BE33C41C92C3B5A0F42A54
Expected Results:	Source disk is unchanged
	src compares qualified equal to dst, src is truncated on dst
	truncation is logged
Actual Results:	Restore anomaly
Analysis:	Expected results not achieved

Case DI-100 for EnCase 3.20	
Case Summary:	Create an image from an XBIOS-IDE source disk to an XBIOS-IDE destination disk and the source contains a FAT16 partition where the source disk is smaller than the destination Introduce an error on the image.
Tester Name:	JRL
Test Date:	Fri Aug 30 04:01:47 2002
PC:	HecRamsey
Disks:	Source: DOS Drive 80 Physical Label F5 Destination: DOS Drive 81 Physical Label none Image media: DOS Drive 80 Physical Label 7C F5 is an IBM-DTLA-307020 with 40188960 sectors 7C is a MAXTOR 6L040J2 with 78177792 sectors CD-ROM with PartitionMagic Pro 6.0 and boot floppy with run scripts FS-TST Release 1.0 CD-ROM + Baddisk 3.2 + Badx13 3.2
Source disk setup:	Dual boot Linux/Windows Me with EXT2 & Fat16 Disk: F5 Host: Cadfael Operator: JRL OS: WindowsMe/Linux Date: Sat Aug 11 11:13:43 2001 DISKWIPE.EXE F5_SRC Cadfael 80 F5 /src X:\pm\pqmagic /cmd=X:\pm\fat-src.txt Load Operating System to Source disk DISKHASH.EXE F5_SRC Cadfael 80 /before Disk hash = 83A0002816BBF089F8BE33C41C92C3B5A0F42A54
Destination Setup:	No destination setup required
Error Setup:	cmd: z:\ss\CORRUPT.EXE DI-100 HecRamsey D:\f5-f16c.e01 8023219 37 Comment: change 16/000/01 to 16/070/01 at LBA 16128
Execute:	Z:\ss\DISKHASH.EXE DI-100 JudgeDee 80 /comment F5(JRL) /new log /after
Log files loc:	test-archive/encase/encase-3.20/DI-100
Log File Highlights:	Image file acquired from DOS Restore environment Windows 2000 EnCase report for case DI-100 is in 100.txt Evidence Number "F5-F16" Alias "F5-F16" File "F:\F5-F16C.E01" was acquired by JRL at 08/30/02 04:07:53AM. The computer system clock read: 08/30/02 04:07:53AM. Evidence acquired under DOS 7.10 using version 3.20. The integrity of the following sector groups could not be verified:16064-16127 Drive Geometry: Total Size 604.0MB (1,236,942 sectors)

Volume "F5-F16" Parameters

File System:	FAT16	Drive Type:	Fixed
Sectors Per Cluster:	32	Bytes Per Sector:	512
Total Sectors:	1,236,942	Total Capacity:	633,126,912 bytes (603.8MB)
Total Clusters:	38,643	Unallocated:	73,105,408 bytes (69.7MB)
Free Clusters:	4,462	Allocated:	560,021,504 bytes (534.1MB)
Volume Name:		Volume Offset:	0
OEM Version:	MSWIN4.1	Volume Serial #:	3B76-451D
Heads:	255	Sectors Per Track:	63
Unused Sectors:	63	Number of FATs:	2
Sectors Per FAT:	151	Boot Sectors:	1

Case DI-100 for EnCase 3.20	
	EnCase Report Case: di-100 Page = = = = Measurement Logs = = = = No compare log found for DI-100 Hash computed for this case (DI-100) Hash after test: 83A0002816BBF089F8BE33C41C92C3B5A0F42A54
Expected Results:	Source disk is unchanged image verification error
Actual Results:	No anomalies
Analysis:	Expected results achieved

Case DI-101 for EnCase 3.20	
Case Summary:	Create an image from an XBIOS-IDE source disk to an XBIOS-IDE destination disk and the source contains a FAT32 partition where the source disk is smaller than the destination
Tester Name:	JRL
Test Date:	Fri Sep 13 20:30:23 2002
PC:	HecRamsey
Disks:	Source: DOS Drive 80 Physical Label A5 Destination: DOS Drive 81 Physical Label A8 Image media: DOS Drive 80 Physical Label 7C A5 is a WDC WD200BB-00AUA1 with 39102336 sectors A8 is a WDC WD200BB-00AUA1 with 39102336 sectors 7C is a MAXTOR 6L040J2 with 78177792 sectors CD-ROM with PartitionMagic Pro 6.0 and boot floppy with run scripts FS-TST Release 1.0 CD-ROM + Baddisk 3.2 + Badx13 3.2
Source disk setup:	Fat32 only Disk: A5 Host: JudgeDee Operator: JRL OS: NoOs Options: none Date: Mon Apr 15 14:35:04 2002 cmd: Z:\ss\DISKWIPE.EXE A5 JudgeDee 80 A5 /src /new_log X:\pm\pqmagic /cmd=X:\pm\f32-src.txt No OS loaded, FAT32 partition only cmd: Z:\ss\DISKHASH.EXE A5 JudgeDee 80 /before /new_log Disk hash = 3DE5C01B5BB337EA3E6CF9BC25EB844F5D00FD14
Destination Setup:	Z:\ss\DISKWIPE.EXE DI-101 HecRamsey 81 A8 /noask /dst /new_log /comment JRL See CMPPTLOG.TXT for partition table
Error Setup:	none
Execute:	Z:\ss\DISKWIPE.EXE DI-101 HecRamsey 81 A8 /noask /dst /new_log /comment JRL Z:\ss\PARTCMP.EXE DI-101 HecRamsey 80 A5 81 A8 /new_log /comment JRL /select 1 1
Log files loc:	test-archive/encase/encase-3.20/DI-101

Log File Highlights:	Source disk Drive 0x80, BIOS: Extensions Present
	Interrupt 13 bios 1022/254/63 (max cyl/hd values)
	Interrupt 13 ext 16383/016/63 (number of cyl/hd)
	39102336 total number of sectors reported via interrupt 13 from the BIOS
	<pre>N Start LBA Length Start C/H/S End C/H/S boot Partition type
	 1 P 000000063 001236942 0000/001/01 0076/254/63 Boot 0B Fat32
	 2 X 001429785 037061955 0089/000/01 1023/254/63 0F extended
	 3 S 000000063 000208782 0089/001/01 0101/254/63 83 Linux
	 4 x 000208845 000144585 0102/000/01 0110/254/63 05 extended
	 5 S 000000063 000144522 0102/001/01 0110/254/63 0B Fat32
	 6 x 000771120 000192780 0137/000/01 0148/254/63 05 extended
	 7 S 000000063 000192717 0137/001/01 0148/254/63 16 other
	 8 S 000000000 000000000 0000/000/00 0000/000/00 00 empty entry
	 9 P 038491740 000064260 1023/000/01 1023/254/63 83 Linux
	10 P 038684520 000417690 1023/000/01 1023/254/63 82 Linux swap</pre>Destination disk Drive 0x81, BIOS: Extensions Present
	Interrupt 13 bios 1022/254/63 (max cyl/hd values)
	Interrupt 13 ext 16383/016/63 (number of cyl/hd)

39102336 total number of sectors reported via interrupt 13 from the BIOS

N		Start LBA	Length	Start C/H/S	End C/H/S	boot	Partition type
1	P	000000063	001333332	0000/001/01	0082/254/63	0B	Fat32
2	P	000000000	000000000	0000/000/00	0000/000/00	00	empty entry
3	P	000000000	000000000	0000/000/00	0000/000/00	00	empty entry
4	P	000000000	000000000	0000/000/00	0000/000/00	00	empty entry

Image file acquired from DOS
Restore environment Windows 2000
EnCase report for case DI-101 is in 101.txt
Evidence Number "A5-f32"   Alias "A5-f32"

File "D:\A5-F32.E01" was acquired by JRL at 09/12/02 11:54:37PM.
The computer system clock read: 09/12/02 11:54:37PM.

Evidence acquired under DOS 7.10 using version 3.20.

File Integrity:
Completely Verified, 0 Errors.
Verification Hash: DD35EAC272F126808184A1B012A49B12

Drive Geometry:
Total Size   604.0MB (1,236,942 sectors)

Volume "A5-f32" Parameters

File System:	FAT32	Drive Type:	Fixed
Sectors Per Cluster:	1	Bytes Per Sector:	512
Total Sectors:	1,236,942	Total Capacity:	623,553,536 bytes (594.7MB)
Total Clusters:	1,217,878	Unallocated:	623,550,464 bytes (594.7MB)
Free Clusters:	1,217,872	Allocated:	3,072 bytes (3.0KB)
Volume Name:		Volume Offset:	0
OEM Version:	MSWIN4.1	Volume Serial #:	0000-0000
Heads:	255	Sectors Per Track:	63
Unused Sectors:	63	Number of FATs:	2
Sectors Per FAT:	9,516	Boot Sectors:	32

EnCase Report
Case: DI-101   Page

= = = = Measurement Logs = = = =
Sectors Compared 1236942
Sectors Differ 3
Diffs range: 1, 32, 9548
Source (1236942) has 96390 fewer sectors than destination (1333332)
Zero fill: 0
Src Byte fill (A5): 0
Dst Byte fill (A8): 0
Other fill: 96390
Other no fill: 0
This case uses the hash computed from case DI-118
Hash after test: 3DE5C01B5BB337EA3E6CF9BC25EB844F5D00FD14

Expected Results:	Source disk is unchanged src compares qualified equal to dst
Actual Results:	Logical restore anomaly
Analysis:	Expected results not achieved

Case DI-108 for EnCase 3.20	
Case Summary:	Create an image from an XBIOS-IDE source disk to an XBIOS-IDE destination disk and the source contains a FAT32 partition

Case DI-108 for EnCase 3.20	
	where the source disk is the same size as the destination Introduce a read error from the source.
Tester Name:	JRL
Test Date:	Tue Sep 10 01:38:11 2002
PC:	HecRamsey
Disks:	Source: DOS Drive 80 Physical Label A5 Destination: DOS Drive 81 Physical Label A8 Image media: DOS Drive 80 Physical Label 7C A5 is a WDC WD200BB-00AUA1 with 39102336 sectors A8 is a WDC WD200BB-00AUA1 with 39102336 sectors 7C is a MAXTOR 6L040J2 with 78177792 sectors CD-ROM with PartitionMagic Pro 6.0 and boot floppy with run scripts FS-TST Release 1.0 CD-ROM + Baddisk 3.2 + Badx13 3.2
Source disk setup:	Fat32 only Disk: A5 Host: JudgeDee Operator: JRL OS: NoOs Options: none Date: Mon Apr 15 14:35:04 2002 cmd: Z:\ss\DISKWIPE.EXE A5 JudgeDee 80 A5 /src /new_log X:\pm\pqmagic /cmd=X:\pm\f32-src.txt No OS loaded, FAT32 partition only cmd: Z:\ss\DISKHASH.EXE A5 JudgeDee 80 /before /new_log Disk hash = 3DE5C01B5BB337EA3E6CF9BC25EB844F5D00FD14
Destination Setup:	Z:\ss\DISKWIPE.EXE DI-108 HecRamsey 81 A8 /noask /dst /new_log /comment JRL See CMPPTLOG.TXT for partition table
Error Setup:	Z:\ss\baddisk 80 5 7 9 2 10 >> A:\err-108.txt Z:\ss\baddisk 80 5 7 9 10 10 >> A:\err-108.txt return code 00010 on command 00002 from disk 00080 at address 00005/00007/00009 return code 00010 on command 00010 from disk 00080 at address 00005/00007/00009
Execute:	Z:\ss\DISKWIPE.EXE DI-108 HecRamsey 81 A8 /noask /dst /new_log /comment JRL Z:\ss\PARTCMP.EXE DI-108 HecRamsey 80 A5 81 A8 /new_log /comment JRL /select 1 1 Z:\ss\DISKHASH.EXE DI-108 Wimsey 80 /comment A5(JRL) /new_log /after
Log files loc:	test-archive/encase/encase-3.20/DI-108
Log File Highlights:	Source disk Drive 0x80, BIOS: Extensions Present Interrupt 13 bios 1022/254/63 (max cyl/hd values) Interrupt 13 ext 16383/016/63 (number of cyl/hd) 39102336 total number of sectors reported via interrupt 13 from the BIOS N Start LBA Length Start C/H/S End C/H/S boot Partition type 1 P 000000063 001236942 0000/001/01 0076/254/63 Boot 0B Fat32 2 X 001429785 037061955 0089/000/01 1023/254/63 0F extended 3 S 000000063 000208782 0089/001/01 0101/254/63 83 Linux 4 x 000208845 000144585 0102/000/01 0110/254/63 05 extended 5 S 000000063 000144522 0102/001/01 0110/254/63 0B Fat32 6 x 000771120 000192780 0137/000/01 0148/254/63 05 extended 7 S 000000063 000192717 0137/001/01 0148/254/63 16 other 8 S 000000000 000000000 0000/000/00 0000/000/00 00 empty entry 9 P 038491740 000064260 1023/000/01 1023/254/63 83 Linux 10 P 038684520 000417690 1023/000/01 1023/254/63 82 Linux swap Destination disk Drive 0x81, BIOS: Extensions Present Interrupt 13 bios 1022/254/63 (max cyl/hd values) Interrupt 13 ext 16383/016/63 (number of cyl/hd) 39102336 total number of sectors reported via interrupt 13 from the BIOS N Start LBA Length Start C/H/S End C/H/S boot Partition type 1 P 000000063 001236942 0000/001/01 0076/254/63 0B Fat32 2 P 000000000 000000000 0000/000/00 0000/000/00 00 empty entry 3 P 000000000 000000000 0000/000/00 0000/000/00 00 empty entry 4 P 000000000 000000000 0000/000/00 0000/000/00 00 empty entry Image file acquired from DOS Restore environment Windows 2000 EnCase report for case DI-108 is in 108.txt Evidence Number "A5-f16-err" Alias "A5-f16-err"

Case DI-108 for EnCase 3.20

File "G:\A5-ERR.E01" was acquired by JRL at 09/10/02 10:14:38PM.
The computer system clock read: 09/10/02 10:14:38PM.

Evidence acquired under DOS 7.10 using version 3.20.

File Integrity:
Completely Verified, 0 Errors.
Verification Hash: 30A8AC0CAAC4D33317AB99ED3380E603

The following sector blocks reported read errors during acquisition:
80704-80767

Drive Geometry:
Total Size   604.0MB (1,236,942 sectors)

Volume "A5-f16-err" Parameters

File System:	FAT32	Drive Type:	Fixed
Sectors Per Cluster:	1	Bytes Per Sector:	512
Total Sectors:	1,236,942	Total Capacity:	623,553,536 bytes (594.7MB)
Total Clusters:	1,217,878	Unallocated:	623,550,464 bytes (594.7MB)
Free Clusters:	1,217,872	Allocated:	3,072 bytes (3.0KB)
Volume Name:		Volume Offset:	0
OEM Version:	MSWIN4.1	Volume Serial #:	0000-0000
Heads:	255	Sectors Per Track:	63
Unused Sectors:	63	Number of FATs:	2
Sectors Per FAT:	9,516	Boot Sectors:	32

EnCase Report
Case: DI-108   Page

= = = = Measurement Logs = = = =
Sectors Compared 1236942
Sectors Differ 60
Diffs range: 1, 32, 9548, 80711-80767
Hash computed for this case (DI-108)
Hash after test: 3DE5C01B5BB337EA3E6CF9BC25EB844F5D00FD14

Expected Results:	Source disk is unchanged
	src compares qualified equal to dst
	error message logged
Actual Results:	Logical restore anomaly
Analysis:	Expected results not achieved

Case DI-112 for EnCase 3.20

Case Summary:	Create an image from an XBIOS-IDE source disk to an XBIOS-IDE destination disk and the source contains a NTFS partition where the source disk is the same size as the destination Introduce an error on the image.
Tester Name:	JRL
Test Date:	Thu Sep 19 07:38:33 2002
PC:	AndWife
Disks:	Source: DOS Drive 80 Physical Label F6 Destination: DOS Drive 81 Physical Label A8 Image media: DOS Drive 80 Physical Label 75 F6 is an IBM-DTLA-307020 with 40188960 sectors A8 is a WDC WD200BB-00AUA1 with 39102336 sectors 75 is a IC35L040AVER07-0 with 80418240 sectors CD-ROM with PartitionMagic Pro 6.0 and boot floppy with run scripts

Case DI-112 for EnCase 3.20	
	FS-TST Release 1.0 CD-ROM + Baddisk 3.2 + Badx13 3.2
Source disk setup:	Windows 2000 with NTFS & Fat32 Disk: F6 Host: Wimsey Operator: JRL OS: Windows 2000 Date: Sat Jul 21 15:53:12 2001 DISKWIPE.EXE F6_SRC Wimsey 80 F6 /src /new_log /noask /comment Windows 2000/NT source X:\pm\pqmagic /cmd=X:\pm\nt-src.txt Load Operating System to Source disk DISKHASH.EXE LX-27 Morse 80 /before Disk hash = 8034683D5D55BA51409AC7B5CB0845CA2CF6B235
Destination Setup:	Z:\ss\DISKWIPE.EXE DI-112 AndWife 81 A8 /noask /dst /new_log /comment JRL No partition table defined
Error Setup:	cmd: Z:\ss\CORRUPT.EXE DI-112 AndWife D:\f6-ntfs.e01 489279 38 Comment: Corrupt NTFS image for DI-112 at 10169/012/01 000010251108 (LBA)
Execute:	Z:\ss\DISKWIPE.EXE DI-112 AndWife 81 A8 /noask /dst /new_log /comment JRL Z:\ss\DISKHASH.EXE DI-112 Wimsey 80 /comment F6(JRL) /new_log /after
Log files loc:	test-archive/encase/encase-3.20/DI-112
Log File Highlights:	Image file acquired from FastBloc Restore environment Windows 2000 EnCase report for case DI-112 is in 112.txt Evidence Number "F6-NTFS" Alias "F6-NTFS" File "D:\F6-NTFS.E01" was acquired by JRL at 09/19/02 08:09:53AM. The computer system clock read: 09/19/02 08:10:27AM. Evidence acquired under Windows 2000 using version 3.20. The integrity of the following sector groups could not be verified:1536-1599 Drive Geometry: Total Size 604.0MB (1,236,940 sectors)

Volume "F6-NTFS" Parameters

File System:	NTFS	Drive Type:	Fixed
Sectors Per Cluster:	2	Bytes Per Sector:	512
Total Sectors:	1,236,940	Total Capacity:	633,313,280 bytes (604.0MB)
Total Clusters:	618,470	Unallocated:	628,548,608 bytes (599.4MB)
Free Clusters:	613,817	Allocated:	4,764,672 bytes (4.5MB)
Volume Name:		Volume Offset:	0

EnCase Report
Case: DI-112   Page

= = = = Measurement Logs = = = =
No compare log found for DI-112
Hash computed for this case (DI-112)
Hash after test: 8034683D5D55BA51409AC7B5CB0845CA2CF6B235

Expected Results:	Source disk is unchanged image verification error
Actual Results:	No anomalies
Analysis:	Expected results achieved

Case DI-118 for EnCase 3.20	
Case Summary:	Create an image from an XBIOS-IDE source disk

Case DI-118 for EnCase 3.20	
	to an XBIOS-IDE destination disk and the source contains a FAT32 partition where the source disk is larger than the destination
Tester Name:	JRL
Test Date:	Thu Sep 12 23:46:21 2002
PC:	HecRamsey
Disks:	Source: DOS Drive 80 Physical Label A5 Destination: DOS Drive 81 Physical Label A8 Image media: DOS Drive 80 Physical Label 7C A5 is a WDC WD200BB-00AUA1 with 39102336 sectors A8 is a WDC WD200BB-00AUA1 with 39102336 sectors 7C is a MAXTOR 6L040J2 with 78177792 sectors CD-ROM with PartitionMagic Pro 6.0 and boot floppy with run scripts FS-TST Release 1.0 CD-ROM + Baddisk 3.2 + Badx13 3.2
Source disk setup:	Fat32 only Disk: A5 Host: JudgeDee Operator: JRL OS: NoOs Options: none Date: Mon Apr 15 14:35:04 2002 cmd: Z:\ss\DISKWIPE.EXE A5 JudgeDee 80 A5 /src /new_log X:\pm\pqmagic /cmd=X:\pm\f32-src.txt No OS loaded, FAT32 partition only cmd: Z:\ss\DISKHASH.EXE A5 JudgeDee 80 /before /new_log Disk hash = 3DE5C01B5BB337EA3E6CF9BC25EB844F5D00FD14
Destination Setup:	Z:\ss\DISKWIPE.EXE DI-118 HecRamsey 81 A8 /noask /dst /new_log /comment JRL See CMPPTLOG.TXT for partition table
Error Setup:	none
Execute:	Z:\ss\DISKWIPE.EXE DI-118 HecRamsey 81 A8 /noask /dst /new_log /comment JRL Z:\ss\PARTCMP.EXE DI-118 HecRamsey 80 A5 81 A8 /new_log /comment JRL /select 1 1 Z:\ss\DISKHASH.EXE DI-118 JudgeDee 80 /comment A5(JRL) /new_log /after
Log files loc:	test-archive/encase/encase-3.20/DI-118
Log File Highlights:	Source disk Drive 0x80, BIOS: Extensions Present Interrupt 13 bios 1022/254/63 (max cyl/hd values) Interrupt 13 ext 16383/016/63 (number of cyl/hd) 39102336 total number of sectors reported via interrupt 13 from the BIOS N Start LBA Length Start C/H/S End C/H/S boot Partition type 1 P 000000063 001236942 0000/001/01 0076/254/63 Boot 0B Fat32 2 X 001429785 037061955 0089/000/01 1023/254/63 0F extended 3 S 000000063 000208782 0089/001/01 0101/254/63 83 Linux 4 x 000208845 000144585 0102/000/01 0110/254/63 05 extended 5 S 000000063 000144522 0102/001/01 0110/254/63 0B Fat32 6 x 000771120 000192780 0137/000/01 0148/254/63 05 extended 7 S 000000063 000192717 0137/001/01 0148/254/63 16 other 8 S 000000000 000000000 0000/000/00 0000/000/00 00 empty entry 9 P 038491740 000064260 1023/000/01 1023/254/63 83 Linux 10 P 038684520 000417690 1023/000/01 1023/254/63 82 Linux swap Destination disk Drive 0x81, BIOS: Extensions Present Interrupt 13 bios 1022/254/63 (max cyl/hd values) Interrupt 13 ext 16383/016/63 (number of cyl/hd) 39102336 total number of sectors reported via interrupt 13 from the BIOS N Start LBA Length Start C/H/S End C/H/S boot Partition type 1 P 000000063 001140552 0000/001/01 0070/254/63 06 Fat16 2 P 000000000 000000000 0000/000/00 0000/000/00 00 empty entry 3 P 000000000 000000000 0000/000/00 0000/000/00 00 empty entry 4 P 000000000 000000000 0000/000/00 0000/000/00 00 empty entry Image file acquired from DOS Restore environment Windows 2000 EnCase report for case DI-118 is in 118.txt Evidence Number "A5-f32" Alias "A5-f32" File "D:\A5-F32.E01" was acquired by JRL at 09/12/02 11:54:37PM. The computer system clock read: 09/12/02 11:54:37PM.

Case DI-118 for EnCase 3.20

Evidence acquired under DOS 7.10 using version 3.20.

File Integrity:
Completely Verified, 0 Errors.
Verification Hash: DD35EAC272F126808184A1B012A49B12

Drive Geometry:
Total Size   604.0MB (1,236,942 sectors)

Volume "A5-f32" Parameters

File System:	FAT32	Drive Type:	Fixed
Sectors Per Cluster:	1	Bytes Per Sector:	512
Total Sectors:	1,236,942	Total Capacity:	623,553,536 bytes (594.7MB)
Total Clusters:	1,217,878	Unallocated:	623,550,464 bytes (594.7MB)
Free Clusters:	1,217,872	Allocated:	3,072 bytes (3.0KB)
Volume Name:		Volume Offset:	0
OEM Version:	MSWIN4.1	Volume Serial #:	0000-0000
Heads:	255	Sectors Per Track:	63
Unused Sectors:	63	Number of FATs:	2
Sectors Per FAT:	9,516	Boot Sectors:	32

EnCase Report
Case: DI-118   Page

= = = = Measurement Logs = = = =
Sectors Compared 1140552
Sectors Differ 3
Diffs range: 1, 32, 9548
Source (1236942) has 96390 more sectors than destination (1140552)
Hash computed for this case (DI-118)
Hash after test: 3DE5C01B5BB337EA3E6CF9BC25EB844F5D00FD14

Expected Results:	Source disk is unchanged src compares qualified equal to dst, src is truncated on dst truncation is logged
Actual Results:	Logical restore anomaly
Analysis:	Expected results not achieved

Case DI-120 for EnCase 3.20

Case Summary:	Create an image from an XBIOS-SCSI source disk to an XBIOS-SCSI destination disk where the source disk is smaller than the destination Introduce an error on the image.
Tester Name:	JRL
Test Date:	Wed Sep 04 01:09:51 2002
PC:	HecRamsey
Disks:	Source: DOS Drive 80 Physical Label E3 Destination: DOS Drive 81 Physical Label none Image media: DOS Drive 80 Physical Label 7C E3 is a QUANTUM ATLAS10K2-TY092J with 17938985 sectors 7C is a MAXTOR 6L040J2 with 78177792 sectors CD-ROM with PartitionMagic Pro 6.0 and boot floppy with run scripts FS-TST Release 1.0 CD-ROM + Baddisk 3.2 + Badx13 3.2
Source disk setup:	Dual boot Linux/Windows Me with EXT2 & Fat16 Disk: E3 Host: Cadfael Operator: JRL OS: Linux Red Hat 7.1/Windows Me Date: Sat Jul 21 16:17:29 2001

Case DI-120 for EnCase 3.20	
	DISKWIPE.EXE E3_SRC Rumpole 80 E3 /src /new_log X:\pm\pqmagic /cmd=X:\pm\fat-src.txt Load Operating System to Source disk DISKHASH.EXE E3_SRC Rumpole 80 /before Disk hash = 0F9DACDA6C63D197C048782003D324108CEC7AB0
Destination Setup:	No destination setup required
Error Setup:	cmd: Z:\ss\CORRUPT.EXE DI-120 HecRamsey C:\e3-all.e02 1044805 51 Comment: Change 255/009/01 to 255/00Q/01 at LBA 40937142
Execute:	Z:\ss\DISKHASH.EXE DI-120 Wimsey 80 /comment E3(JRL) /new_log /after
Log files loc:	test-archive/encase/encase-3.20/DI-120
Log File Highlights:	Image file acquired from DOS Restore environment Windows 2000 EnCase report for case DI-120 is in 120.txt Evidence Number "E3-all" Alias "E3-all" File "F:\E3-ALL.E01" was acquired by JRL at 09/04/02 01:15:13AM. The computer system clock read: 09/04/02 01:15:13AM. Evidence acquired under DOS 7.10 using version 3.20. The integrity of the following sector groups could not be verified:4097088-4097151 Drive Geometry: Total Size 8.6GB (17,938,985 sectors) Partitions: | Code	Type	Start Sector	Total Sectors	Size
---	---	---	---	---
06	BIGDOS	0	1237005	604.0MB
83	Linux EXT2	9430155	6152895	2.9GB
82	Linux Swap	17510850	417690	204.0MB
83	Linux EXT2	2249100	208845	102.0MB
06	BIGDOS	2457945	144585	70.6MB
16	HiddenFAT16	6699105	192780	94.1MB	 EnCase Report Case: DI-120 Page = = = = Measurement Logs = = = = No compare log found for DI-120 Hash computed for this case (DI-120) Hash after test: 0F9DACDA6C63D197C048782003D324108CEC7AB0
Expected Results:	Source disk is unchanged image verification error
Actual Results:	No anomalies
Analysis:	Expected results achieved

Case DI-121 for EnCase 3.20	
Case Summary:	Create an image from an XBIOS-SCSI source disk to an XBIOS-SCSI destination disk where the source disk is smaller than the destination
Tester Name:	JRL
Test Date:	Sun May 26 05:55:30 2002
PC:	Paladin
Disks:	Source: DOS Drive 80 Physical Label E4 Destination: DOS Drive 81 Physical Label 11 Image media: DOS Drive 80 Physical Label 7C E4 is a QUANTUM ATLAS10K2-TY092J with 17938985 sectors 11 is a FUJITSU MAN3184MC with 35885447 sectors 7C is a MAXTOR 6L040J2 with 78177792 sectors CD-ROM with PartitionMagic Pro 6.0 and boot floppy with run scripts FS-TST Release 1.0 CD-ROM + Baddisk 3.2 + Badx13 3.2
Source disk setup:	Windows 2000 with NTFS & Fat32 Disk: E4 Host: JudgeDee

	Operator: JRL OS: Windows 2000/NT Date: Sat Jul 21 16:58:28 2001 DISKWIPE.EXE E4_SRC JudgeDee 80 E4 /src /noask /comment Windows 2000 source disk X:\pm\pqmagic /cmd=X:\pm\nt-src.txt Load Operating System to Source disk cmd: X:\ss\DISKHASH.EXE Hash Wimsey 80 /comment E4 /new_log /before Disk hash = 25BF8AF6B2D3E0BD1909C96E368DB27F51C49CBF
Destination Setup:	Z:\ss\DISKWIPE.EXE DI-121 Paladin 81 11 /noask /dst /new_log /comment JRL No partition table defined
Error Setup:	none
Execute:	Z:\ss\DISKWIPE.EXE DI-121 Paladin 81 11 /noask /dst /new_log /comment JRL Z:\ss\DISKCMP.EXE DI-121 Wimsey 80 E4 81 11 /new_log /comment JRL Z:\ss\DISKHASH.EXE DI-121 Wimsey 80 /comment E4(JRL) /new_log /after
Log files loc:	test-archive/encase/encase-3.20/DI-121
Log File Highlights:	Image file acquired from DOS Restore environment Windows 2000 EnCase report for case DI-121 is in E4.txt Evidence Number "1" Alias "E4 image" File "D:\E4.E01" was acquired by JRL at 05/25/02 04:43:12PM. The computer system clock read: 05/25/02 04:43:12PM. Evidence acquired under DOS 7.10 using version 3.20. File Integrity: Completely Verified, 0 Errors. Verification Hash: AA49F2184A3A4256117B33D906CF7884 Drive Geometry: Total Size 8.6GB (17,938,985 sectors) Partitions: {{PARTITION_TABLE}} EnCase Report Case: E4 Page = = = = Measurement Logs = = = = Sectors Compared 17938985 Sectors Differ 0 Diffs range Source (17938985) has 17946463 fewer sectors than destination (35885448) Zero fill: 0 Src Byte fill (E4): 0 Dst Byte fill (11): 17946463 Other fill: 0 Other no fill: 0 Hash computed for this case (DI-121) Hash after test: 25BF8AF6B2D3E0BD1909C96E368DB27F51C49CBF
Expected Results:	Source disk is unchanged src compares qualified equal to dst
Actual Results:	No anomalies
Analysis:	Expected results achieved

Partition table (from Log File Highlights):

Code	Type	Start Sector	Total Sectors	Size
0B	FAT32	0	6152895	2.9GB
07	NTFS	10249470	1237005	604.0MB
17	Hidden IFS	13542795	1638630	800.1MB
1B	HiddenFAT32	16691535	1237005	604.0MB

Case DI-122 for EnCase 3.20	
Case Summary:	Create an image from an XBIOS-SCSI source disk to an XBIOS-SCSI destination disk where the source disk is the same size as the destination Introduce a read error from the source.
Tester Name:	JRL
Test Date:	Sat Sep 07 21:19:12 2002
PC:	HecRamsey
Disks:	Source: DOS Drive 80 Physical Label E4 Destination: DOS Drive 81 Physical Label E2 Image media: DOS Drive 80 Physical Label 7C E4 is a QUANTUM ATLAS10K2-TY092J with 17938985 sectors E2 is a QUANTUM ATLAS10K2-TY092J with 17938985 sectors 7C is a MAXTOR 6L040J2 with 78177792 sectors CD-ROM with PartitionMagic Pro 6.0 and boot floppy with run scripts FS-TST Release 1.0 CD-ROM + Baddisk 3.2 + Badx13 3.2
Source disk setup:	Windows 2000 with NTFS & Fat32 Disk: E4 Host: JudgeDee Operator: JRL OS: Windows 2000/NT Date: Sat Jul 21 16:58:28 2001 DISKWIPE.EXE E4_SRC JudgeDee 80 E4 /src /noask /comment Windows 2000 source disk X:\pm\pqmagic /cmd=X:\pm\nt-src.txt Load Operating System to Source disk cmd: X:\ss\DISKHASH.EXE Hash Wimsey 80 /comment E4 /new_log /before Disk hash = 25BF8AF6B2D3E0BD1909C96E368DB27F51C49CBF
Destination Setup:	Z:\ss\DISKWIPE.EXE DI-122 HecRamsey 81 E2 /noask /dst /new_log /comment JRL No partition table defined
Error Setup:	Z:\ss\badx13 81 42 10 5938247 > a:\err-122.txt Return error code 10 for X13 command 42 from drive 81 at LBA sector 5,938,247
Execute:	Z:\ss\DISKWIPE.EXE DI-122 HecRamsey 81 E2 /noask /dst /new_log /comment JRL Z:\ss\DISKCMP.EXE DI-122 McCloud 80 E4 81 E2 /new_log /comment JRL Z:\ss\DISKHASH.EXE DI-122 McCloud 80 /comment E4(JRL) /new_log /after
Log files loc:	test-archive/encase/encase-3.20/DI-122
Log File Highlights:	Image file acquired from DOS Restore environment Windows 2000 EnCase report for case DI-122 is in 122.txt Evidence Number "E4-err" Alias "E4-err" File "D:\E4-ERR.E01" was acquired by JRL at 09/07/02 10:11:04PM. The computer system clock read: 09/07/02 10:11:04PM. Evidence acquired under DOS 7.10 using version 3.20. File Integrity: Completely Verified, 0 Errors. Verification Hash: 438D79095C0E3ED7CC6600A47DBC879F The following sector blocks reported read errors during acquisition: 5938240-5938303 Drive Geometry: Total Size 8.6GB (17,938,985 sectors)

Partitions:

Code	Type	Start Sector	Total Sectors	Size
0B	FAT32	0	6152895	2.9GB
07	NTFS	10249470	1237005	604.0MB
17	Hidden IFS	13542795	1638630	800.1MB
1B	HiddenFAT32	16691535	1237005	604.0MB

Case DI-122 for EnCase 3.20	
	EnCase Report Case: DI-122 Page = = = = Measurement Logs = = = = Sectors Compared 17938985 Sectors Differ 10502 Diffs range 5938247-5938303, 17928540-17938984 Hash computed for this case (DI-122) Hash after test: 25BF8AF6B2D3E0BD1909C96E368DB27F51C49CBF
Expected Results:	Source disk is unchanged src compares qualified equal to dst error message logged
Actual Results:	Restore anomaly
Analysis:	Expected results not achieved

Case DI-127 for EnCase 3.20	
Case Summary:	Create an image from an XBIOS-SCSI source disk to an XBIOS-SCSI destination disk where the source disk is the same size as the destination
Tester Name:	JRL
Test Date:	Sat May 25 17:16:28 2002
PC:	Wimsey
Disks:	Source: DOS Drive 80 Physical Label E4 Destination: DOS Drive 81 Physical Label E1 Image media: DOS Drive 80 Physical Label 7C E4 is a QUANTUM ATLAS10K2-TY092J with 17938985 sectors E1 is a QUANTUM ATLAS10K2-TY092J with 17938985 sectors 7C is a MAXTOR 6L040J2 with 78177792 sectors CD-ROM with PartitionMagic Pro 6.0 and boot floppy with run scripts FS-TST Release 1.0 CD-ROM + Baddisk 3.2 + Badx13 3.2
Source disk setup:	Windows 2000 with NTFS & Fat32 Disk: E4 Host: JudgeDee Operator: JRL OS: Windows 2000/NT Date: Sat Jul 21 16:58:28 2001 DISKWIPE.EXE E4_SRC JudgeDee 80 E4 /src /noask /comment Windows 2000 source disk X:\pm\pqmagic /cmd=X:\pm\nt-src.txt Load Operating System to Source disk cmd: X:\ss\DISKHASH.EXE Hash Wimsey 80 /comment E4 /new_log /before Disk hash = 25BF8AF6B2D3E0BD1909C96E368DB27F51C49CBF
Destination Setup:	Z:\ss\DISKWIPE.EXE DI-127 Wimsey 81 E1 /noask /dst /new_log /comment JRL No partition table defined
Error Setup:	none
Execute:	Z:\ss\DISKWIPE.EXE DI-127 Wimsey 81 E1 /noask /dst /new_log /comment JRL Z:\ss\DISKCMP.EXE DI-127 Wimsey 80 E4 81 E1 /new_log /comment JRL
Log files loc:	test-archive/encase/encase-3.20/DI-127
Log File Highlights:	Image file acquired from DOS Restore environment Windows 2000 EnCase report for case DI-127 is in E4.txt Evidence Number "1" Alias "E4 image" File "D:\E4.E01" was acquired by JRL at 05/25/02 04:43:12PM. The computer system clock read: 05/25/02 04:43:12PM. Evidence acquired under DOS 7.10 using version 3.20. File Integrity: Completely Verified, 0 Errors. Verification Hash: AA49F2184A3A4256117B33D906CF7884 Drive Geometry: Total Size 8.6GB (17,938,985 sectors)

Case DI-127 for EnCase 3.20

	Partitions:				
	Code	Type	Start Sector	Total Sectors	Size
	0B	FAT32	0	6152895	2.9GB
	07	NTFS	10249470	1237005	604.0MB
	17	Hidden IFS	13542795	1638630	800.1MB
	1B	HiddenFAT32	16691535	1237005	604.0MB

```
EnCase Report
Case: E4          Page

= = = = Measurement Logs = = = =
Sectors Compared 17938985
Sectors Differ 10445
Diffs range 17928540-17938984
This case uses the hash computed from case DI-121
Hash after test: 25BF8AF6B2D3E0BD1909C96E368DB27F51C49CBF
```

Expected Results:	Source disk is unchanged src compares equal to dst
Actual Results:	Restore anomaly
Analysis:	Expected results not achieved

Case DI-128 for EnCase 3.20

Case Summary:	Create an image from an XBIOS-SCSI source disk to an XBIOS-SCSI destination disk where the source disk is larger than the destination
Tester Name:	JRL
Test Date:	Sat Jun 01 09:41:58 2002
PC:	Rumpole
Disks:	Source: DOS Drive 80 Physical Label E4 Destination: DOS Drive 81 Physical Label EB Image media: DOS Drive 80 Physical Label 7C E4 is a QUANTUM ATLAS10K2-TY092J with 17938985 sectors EB is a SEAGATE ST39204LC with 17921835 sectors 7C is a MAXTOR 6L040J2 with 78177792 sectors CD-ROM with PartitionMagic Pro 6.0 and boot floppy with run scripts FS-TST Release 1.0 CD-ROM + Baddisk 3.2 + Badx13 3.2
Source disk setup:	Windows 2000 with NTFS & Fat32 Disk: E4 Host: JudgeDee Operator: JRL OS: Windows 2000/NT Date: Sat Jul 21 16:58:28 2001 DISKWIPE.EXE E4_SRC JudgeDee 80 E4 /src /noask /comment Windows 2000 source disk X:\pm\pqmagic /cmd=X:\pm\nt-src.txt Load Operating System to Source disk cmd: X:\ss\DISKHASH.EXE Hash Wimsey 80 /comment E4 /new_log /before Disk hash = 25BF8AF6B2D3E0BD1909C96E368DB27F51C49CBF
Destination Setup:	Z:\ss\DISKWIPE.EXE DI-128 Rumpole 81 EB /noask /dst /new_log /comment JRL No partition table defined
Error Setup:	none
Execute:	Z:\ss\DISKWIPE.EXE DI-128 Rumpole 81 EB /noask /dst /new_log /comment JRL Z:\ss\DISKCMP.EXE DI-128 Wimsey 80 E4 81 EB /new_log /comment JRL
Log files loc:	test-archive/encase/encase-3.20/DI-128
Log File Highlights:	Image file acquired from DOS Restore environment Windows 2000 EnCase report for case DI-128 is in E4.txt Evidence Number "1" Alias "E4 image" File "D:\E4.E01" was acquired by JRL at 05/25/02 04:43:12PM. The computer system clock read: 05/25/02 04:43:12PM. Evidence acquired under DOS 7.10 using version 3.20.

Case DI-128 for EnCase 3.20	
	File Integrity: Completely Verified, 0 Errors. Verification Hash: AA49F2184A3A4256117B33D906CF7884 Drive Geometry: Total Size 8.6GB (17,938,985 sectors) Partitions:

Code	Type	Start Sector	Total Sectors	Size
0B	FAT32	0	6152895	2.9GB
07	NTFS	10249470	1237005	604.0MB
17	Hidden IFS	13542795	1638630	800.1MB
1B	HiddenFAT32	16691535	1237005	604.0MB

	EnCase Report Case: E4 Page = = = = Measurement Logs = = = = Sectors Compared 17921835 Sectors Differ 9360 Diffs range 17912475-17921834 Source (17938985) has 17150 more sectors than destination (17921835) This case uses the hash computed from case DI-121 Hash after test: 25BF8AF6B2D3E0BD1909C96E368DB27F51C49CBF
Expected Results:	Source disk is unchanged src compares qualified equal to dst, src is truncated on dst truncation is logged
Actual Results:	Restore anomaly
Analysis:	Expected results not achieved

Case DI-129 for EnCase 3.20	
Case Summary:	Create an image from an XBIOS-SCSI source disk to an XBIOS-SCSI destination disk and the source contains a FAT16 partition where the source disk is smaller than the destination Introduce an error on the image.
Tester Name:	JRL
Test Date:	Fri Aug 30 20:57:12 2002
PC:	HecRamsey
Disks:	Source: DOS Drive 80 Physical Label E3 Destination: DOS Drive 81 Physical Label none Image media: DOS Drive 80 Physical Label 7C E3 is a QUANTUM ATLAS10K2-TY092J with 17938985 sectors 7C is a MAXTOR 6L040J2 with 78177792 sectors CD-ROM with PartitionMagic Pro 6.0 and boot floppy with run scripts FS-TST Release 1.0 CD-ROM + Baddisk 3.2 + Badx13 3.2
Source disk setup:	Dual boot Linux/Windows Me with EXT2 & Fat16 Disk: E3 Host: Cadfael Operator: JRL OS: Linux Red Hat 7.1/Windows Me Date: Sat Jul 21 16:17:29 2001 DISKWIPE.EXE E3_SRC Rumpole 80 E3 /src /new_log X:\pm\pqmagic /cmd=X:\pm\fat-src.txt Load Operating System to Source disk DISKHASH.EXE E3_SRC Rumpole 80 /before Disk hash = 0F9DACDA6C63D197C048782003D324108CEC7AB0
Destination Setup:	No destination setup required
Error Setup:	cmd: Z:\ss\CORRUPT.EXE DI-129 HecRamsey C:\e3-f16c.e01 8237267 37 Comment: Change 1/007/44 to 1/077/44 at LBA 16549
Execute:	Z:\ss\DISKHASH.EXE DI-129 Cadfael 80 /comment E3(JRL) /new_log /after
Log files loc:	test-archive/encase/encase-3.20/DI-129
Log File	Image file acquired from DOS

Case DI-129 for EnCase 3.20

Highlights:	Restore environment Windows 2000 EnCase report for case DI-129 is in 129.txt Evidence Number "E3-F16" Alias "E3-F16" File "F:\E3-F16C.E01" was acquired by JRL at 08/30/02 09:21:28PM. The computer system clock read: 08/30/02 09:21:28PM. Evidence acquired under DOS 7.10 using version 3.20. The integrity of the following sector groups could not be verified:16448-16511 Drive Geometry: Total Size 604.0MB (1,236,942 sectors)

Volume "E3-F16" Parameters

File System:	FAT16	Drive Type:	Fixed
Sectors Per Cluster:	32	Bytes Per Sector:	512
Total Sectors:	1,236,942	Total Capacity:	633,126,912 bytes (603.8MB)
Total Clusters:	38,643	Unallocated:	85,213,184 bytes (81.3MB)
Free Clusters:	5,201	Allocated:	547,913,728 bytes (522.5MB)
Volume Name:		Volume Offset:	0
OEM Version:	MSWIN4.1	Volume Serial #:	3B65-7909
Heads:	255	Sectors Per Track:	63
Unused Sectors:	63	Number of FATs:	2
Sectors Per FAT:	151	Boot Sectors:	1

	EnCase Report Case: DI-129 Page = = = = Measurement Logs = = = = No compare log found for DI-129 Hash computed for this case (DI-129) Hash after test: 0F9DACDA6C63D197C048782003D324108CEC7AB0
Expected Results:	Source disk is unchanged image verification error
Actual Results:	No anomalies
Analysis:	Expected results achieved

Case DI-130 for EnCase 3.20

Case Summary:	Create an image from an XBIOS-SCSI source disk to an XBIOS-SCSI destination disk and the source contains a FAT32 partition where the source disk is smaller than the destination
Tester Name:	JRL
Test Date:	Tue Jun 11 08:11:19 2002
PC:	Wimsey
Disks:	Source: DOS Drive 80 Physical Label E4 Destination: DOS Drive 81 Physical Label 11 Image media: DOS Drive 80 Physical Label 7C E4 is a QUANTUM ATLAS10K2-TY092J with 17938985 sectors 11 is a FUJITSU MAN3184MC with 35885447 sectors 7C is a MAXTOR 6L040J2 with 78177792 sectors CD-ROM with PartitionMagic Pro 6.0 and boot floppy with run scripts FS-TST Release 1.0 CD-ROM + Baddisk 3.2 + Badx13 3.2
Source disk setup:	Windows 2000 with NTFS & Fat32 Disk: E4 Host: JudgeDee

	Operator: JRL OS: Windows 2000/NT Date: Sat Jul 21 16:58:28 2001 DISKWIPE.EXE E4_SRC JudgeDee 80 E4 /src /noask /comment Windows 2000 source disk X:\pm\pqmagic /cmd=X:\pm\nt-src.txt Load Operating System to Source disk cmd: X:\ss\DISKHASH.EXE Hash Wimsey 80 /comment E4 /new_log /before Disk hash = 25BF8AF6B2D3E0BD1909C96E368DB27F51C49CBF
Destination Setup:	Z:\ss\DISKWIPE.EXE DI-130 Wimsey 81 11 /noask /dst /new_log /comment JRL See CMPPTLOG.TXT for partition table
Error Setup:	none
Execute:	Z:\ss\DISKWIPE.EXE DI-130 Wimsey 81 11 /noask /dst /new_log /comment JRL Z:\ss\PARTCMP.EXE DI-130 Wimsey 80 E4 81 11 /new_log /comment JRL /select 1 1 Z:\ss\DISKHASH.EXE DI-130 Wimsey 80 /comment E4(JRL) /new_log /after
Log files loc:	test-archive/encase/encase-3.20/DI-130

Log File Highlights:	Source disk Drive 0x80, BIOS: Extensions Present
	Interrupt 13 bios 1022/254/63 (max cyl/hd values)
	Interrupt 13 ext 01023/255/63 (number of cyl/hd)
	17938985 total number of sectors reported via interrupt 13 from the BIOS
	<pre>N Start LBA Length Start C/H/S End C/H/S boot Partition type
	 1 P 000000063 006152832 0000/001/01 0382/254/63 Boot 0B Fat32
	 2 X 008193150 009735390 0510/000/01 1023/254/63 0F extended
	 3 S 000000000 000000000 0000/000/00 0000/000/00 00 empty entry
	 4 x 002056320 001237005 0638/000/01 0714/254/63 05 extended
	 5 S 000000063 001236942 0638/001/01 0714/254/63 07 NTFS
	 6 x 005349645 001638630 0843/000/01 0944/254/63 05 extended
	 7 S 000000063 001638567 0843/001/01 0944/254/63 17 other
	 8 x 008498385 001237005 1023/000/01 1023/254/63 05 extended
	 9 S 000000063 001236942 1023/001/01 1023/254/63 1B other
	10 S 000000000 000000000 0000/000/00 0000/000/00 00 empty entry
	11 P 000000000 000000000 0000/000/00 0000/000/00 00 empty entry
	12 P 000000000 000000000 0000/000/00 0000/000/00 00 empty entry</pre>Destination disk Drive 0x81, BIOS: Extensions Present
	Interrupt 13 bios 1022/254/63 (max cyl/hd values)
	Interrupt 13 ext 01023/255/63 (number of cyl/hd)
	35885448 total number of sectors reported via interrupt 13 from the BIOS
	<pre>N Start LBA Length Start C/H/S End C/H/S boot Partition type
	 1 P 000000063 006361677 0000/001/01 0395/254/63 0B Fat32
	 2 P 000000000 000000000 0000/000/00 0000/000/00 00 empty entry
	 3 P 000000000 000000000 0000/000/00 0000/000/00 00 empty entry
	 4 P 000000000 000000000 0000/000/00 0000/000/00 00 empty entry</pre>Image file acquired from DOS
	Restore environment Windows 2000
	EnCase report for case DI-130 is in E4-fat32.txt
	Evidence Number "1" Alias "1"
	
	File "D:\E4-FAT32.E01" was acquired by JRL at 06/11/02 04:50:21PM.
	The computer system clock read: 06/11/02 04:50:21PM.
	
	Evidence acquired under DOS 7.10 using version 3.20.
	
	File Integrity:
	Completely Verified, 0 Errors.
	Verification Hash: 25B37B7DFDDFACB085841B6686FA642E
	
	Drive Geometry:
	Total Size 2.9GB (6,152,832 sectors)

Case DI-130 for EnCase 3.20

Volume "1" Parameters

File System:	FAT32	Drive Type:	Fixed
Sectors Per Cluster:	4	Bytes Per Sector:	512
Total Sectors:	6,152,832	Total Capacity:	3,137,974,272 bytes (2.9GB)
Total Clusters:	1,532,214	Unallocated:	1,684,680,704 bytes (1.6GB)
Free Clusters:	822,598	Allocated:	1,453,293,568 bytes (1.4GB)
Volume Name:		Volume Offset:	0
OEM Version:	MSWIN4.1	Volume Serial #:	0000-0000
Heads:	255	Sectors Per Track:	63
Unused Sectors:	63	Number of FATs:	2
Sectors Per FAT:	11,972	Boot Sectors:	32

```
EnCase Report
Case: E4-FAT32 Page

= = = = Measurement Logs = = = =
Sectors Compared 6152832
Sectors Differ 1
Diffs range:  1
Source (6152832) has 208845 fewer sectors than destination (6361677)
Zero fill:     0
Src Byte fill (E4): 0
Dst Byte fill (11): 208845
Other fill:    0
Other no fill: 0
Hash computed for this case (DI-130)
Hash after test: 25BF8AF6B2D3E0BD1909C96E368DB27F51C49CBF
```

Expected Results:	Source disk is unchanged src compares qualified equal to dst
Actual Results:	Logical restore anomaly
Analysis:	Expected results not achieved

Case DI-137 for EnCase 3.20

Case Summary:	Create an image from an XBIOS-SCSI source disk to an XBIOS-SCSI destination disk and the source contains a FAT16 partition where the source disk is the same size as the destination Introduce a read error from the source.
Tester Name:	JRL
Test Date:	Tue Sep 10 09:11:52 2002
PC:	Cadfael
Disks:	Source: DOS Drive 80 Physical Label E3 Destination: DOS Drive 81 Physical Label E6 Image media: DOS Drive 80 Physical Label 70 E3 is a QUANTUM ATLAS10K2-TY092J with 17938985 sectors E6 is a SEAGATE ST318404LC with 35843670 sectors 70 is a IC35L040AVER07-0 with 80418240 sectors CD-ROM with PartitionMagic Pro 6.0 and boot floppy with run scripts FS-TST Release 1.0 CD-ROM + Baddisk 3.2 + Badx13 3.2
Source disk setup:	Dual boot Linux/Windows Me with EXT2 & Fat16 Disk: E3 Host: Cadfael Operator: JRL OS: Linux Red Hat 7.1/Windows Me Date: Sat Jul 21 16:17:29 2001 DISKWIPE.EXE E3_SRC Rumpole 80 E3 /src /new_log X:\pm\pqmagic /cmd=X:\pm\fat-src.txt Load Operating System to Source disk DISKHASH.EXE E3_SRC Rumpole 80 /before

	Disk hash = 0F9DACDA6C63D197C048782003D324108CEC7AB0
Destination Setup:	Z:\ss\DISKWIPE.EXE DI-137 Cadfael 81 E6 /noask /dst /new_log /comment JRL
	See CMPPTLOG.TXT for partition table
Error Setup:	Z:\ss\baddisk 81 9 13 61 2 10 >> A:\err-137.txt
	Z:\ss\baddisk 81 9 13 61 10 10 >> A:\err-137.txt
	return code 00010 on command 00002 from disk 00081
	at address 00009/00013/00061
	return code 00010 on command 00010 from disk 00081
	at address 00009/00013/00061
Execute:	Z:\ss\DISKWIPE.EXE DI-137 Cadfael 81 E6 /noask /dst /new_log /comment JRL
	Z:\ss\PARTCMP.EXE DI-137 Cadfael 80 E3 81 E6 /new_log /comment JRL /select 1 1
	Z:\ss\DISKHASH.EXE DI-137 Cadfael 80 /comment E3(JRL) /new_log /after
Log files loc:	test-archive/encase/encase-3.20/DI-137
Log File Highlights:	Source disk Drive 0x80, BIOS: Extensions Present

```
Source disk Drive 0x80, BIOS: Extensions Present
Interrupt 13  bios  1022/254/63 (max cyl/hd values)
Interrupt 13  ext   01023/255/63 (number of cyl/hd)
17938985 total number of sectors reported via interrupt 13 from the
BIOS
 N   Start LBA Length    Start C/H/S End C/H/S  boot Partition type
 1 P 000000063 001236942 0000/001/01 0076/254/63 Boot 06 Fat16
 2 X 002249100 007181055 0140/000/01 0586/254/63      05 extended
 3 S 000000063 000208782 0140/001/01 0152/254/63      83 Linux
 4 x 000208845 000144585 0153/000/01 0161/254/63      05 extended
 5 S 000000063 000144522 0153/001/01 0161/254/63      06 Fat16
 6 x 004450005 000192780 0417/000/01 0428/254/63      05 extended
 7 S 000000063 000192717 0417/001/01 0428/254/63      16 other
 8 S 000000000 000000000 0000/000/00 0000/000/00      00 empty entry
 9 P 009430155 006152895 0587/000/01 0969/254/63      83 Linux
10 P 017510850 000417690 1023/000/01 1023/254/63      82 Linux swap
Destination disk Drive 0x81, BIOS: Extensions Present
Interrupt 13  bios  1022/254/63 (max cyl/hd values)
Interrupt 13  ext   01023/255/63 (number of cyl/hd)
35843670 total number of sectors reported via interrupt 13 from the
BIOS
 N   Start LBA Length    Start C/H/S End C/H/S  boot Partition type
 1 P 000000063 001236942 0000/001/01 0076/254/63      06 Fat16
 2 P 000000000 000000000 0000/000/00 0000/000/00      00 empty entry
 3 P 000000000 000000000 0000/000/00 0000/000/00      00 empty entry
 4 P 000000000 000000000 0000/000/00 0000/000/00      00 empty entry
Image file acquired from DOS
Restore environment Windows 2000
EnCase report for case DI-137 is in 137.txt
Evidence Number "E3-f16-err"   Alias "E3-f16-err"

File "D:\E3-ERR.E01" was acquired by JRL at 09/10/02 10:56:57AM.
The computer system clock read: 09/10/02 10:56:57AM.

Evidence acquired under DOS 7.10 using version 3.20.

File Integrity:
Completely Verified, 0 Errors.
Verification Hash:    AE05295683A3B960728A83C599652EAA

The following sector blocks reported read errors during acquisition:
145344-145407

Drive Geometry:
Total Size      604.0MB (1,236,942 sectors)
```

Case DI-137 for EnCase 3.20

Volume "E3-f16-err" Parameters

File System:	FAT16	Drive Type:	Fixed
Sectors Per Cluster:	32	Bytes Per Sector:	512
Total Sectors:	1,236,942	Total Capacity:	633,126,912 bytes (603.8MB)
Total Clusters:	38,643	Unallocated:	85,213,184 bytes (81.3MB)
Free Clusters:	5,201	Allocated:	547,913,728 bytes (522.5MB)
Volume Name:		Volume Offset:	0
OEM Version:	MSWIN4.1	Volume Serial #:	3B65-7909
Heads:	255	Sectors Per Track:	63
Unused Sectors:	63	Number of FATs:	2
Sectors Per FAT:	151	Boot Sectors:	1

EnCase Report
Case: DI-137   Page

= = = = Measurement Logs = = = =
Sectors Compared 1236942
Sectors Differ 7
Diffs range: 145401-145407
Hash computed for this case (DI-137)
Hash after test: 0F9DACDA6C63D197C048782003D324108CEC7AB0

Expected Results:	Source disk is unchanged src compares qualified equal to dst error message logged
Actual Results:	No anomalies
Analysis:	Expected results achieved

Case DI-140 for EnCase 3.20

Case Summary:	Create an image from an XBIOS-SCSI source disk to an XBIOS-SCSI destination disk and the source contains a FAT16 partition where the source disk is the same size as the destination Introduce a write error writing to the image.
Tester Name:	JRL
Test Date:	Wed Sep 11 04:50:56 2002
PC:	HecRamsey
Disks:	Source: DOS Drive 80 Physical Label E3 Destination: DOS Drive 81 Physical Label E2 Image media: DOS Drive 80 Physical Label CC E3 is a QUANTUM ATLAS10K2-TY092J with 17938985 sectors E2 is a QUANTUM ATLAS10K2-TY092J with 17938985 sectors CC is a SEAGATE ST336705LC with 71687370 sectors CD-ROM with PartitionMagic Pro 6.0 and boot floppy with run scripts FS-TST Release 1.0 CD-ROM + Baddisk 3.2 + Badx13 3.2
Source disk setup:	Dual boot Linux/Windows Me with EXT2 & Fat16 Disk: E3 Host: Cadfael Operator: JRL OS: Linux Red Hat 7.1/Windows Me Date: Sat Jul 21 16:17:29 2001 DISKWIPE.EXE E3_SRC Rumpole 80 E3 /src /new_log X:\pm\pqmagic /cmd=X:\pm\fat-src.txt Load Operating System to Source disk DISKHASH.EXE E3_SRC Rumpole 80 /before Disk hash = 0F9DACDA6C63D197C048782003D324108CEC7AB0
Destination Setup:	No destination setup required
Error Setup:	Z:\ss\baddisk 81 4 10 14 3 10 >> A:\err-140.txt return code 00010 on command 00003 from disk 00081

Case DI-140 for EnCase 3.20	
	at address 00004/00010/00014
Execute:	
Log files loc:	test-archive/encase/encase-3.20/DI-140
Log File Highlights:	Image file acquired from DOS Restore environment Windows 2000 EnCase report for case DI-140 is in NOLOG.txt Message displayed during DOS acquire: Error in <file name> cannot write to this file = = = = = Measurement Logs = = = = No compare log found for DI-140 This case uses the hash computed from case DI-142 Hash after test: 0F9DACDA6C63D197C048782003D324108CEC7AB0
Expected Results:	Source disk is unchanged error message logged
Actual Results:	No anomalies
Analysis:	Expected results achieved

Case DI-141 for EnCase 3.20	
Case Summary:	Create an image from an XBIOS-SCSI source disk to an XBIOS-SCSI destination disk and the source contains a FAT32 partition where the source disk is the same size as the destination Introduce an error on the image.
Tester Name:	JRL
Test Date:	Fri Aug 30 23:31:27 2002
PC:	HecRamsey
Disks:	Source: DOS Drive 80 Physical Label E4 Destination: DOS Drive 81 Physical Label none Image media: DOS Drive 80 Physical Label 7C E4 is a QUANTUM ATLAS10K2-TY092J with 17938985 sectors 7C is a MAXTOR 6L040J2 with 78177792 sectors CD-ROM with PartitionMagic Pro 6.0 and boot floppy with run scripts FS-TST Release 1.0 CD-ROM + Baddisk 3.2 + Badx13 3.2
Source disk setup:	Windows 2000 with NTFS & Fat32 Disk: E4 Host: JudgeDee Operator: JRL OS: Windows 2000/NT Date: Sat Jul 21 16:58:28 2001 DISKWIPE.EXE E4_SRC JudgeDee 80 E4 /src /noask /comment Windows 2000 source disk X:\pm\pqmagic /cmd=X:\pm\nt-src.txt Load Operating System to Source disk cmd: X:\ss\DISKHASH.EXE Hash Wimsey 80 /comment E4 /new_log /before Disk hash = 25BF8AF6B2D3E0BD1909C96E368DB27F51C49CBF
Destination Setup:	No destination setup required
Error Setup:	cmd: Z:\ss\CORRUPT.EXE DI-141 HecRamsey C:\e4-f32c.e02 656147 5A Comment: Change 255/001/01 to 255/Z01/01 at LBA 4096638??
Execute:	Z:\ss\DISKHASH.EXE DI-141 Rumpole 80 /comment E4(JRL) /new_log /after
Log files loc:	test-archive/encase/encase-3.20/DI-141
Log File Hihlights:	Image file acquired from DOS Restore environment Windows 2000 EnCase report for case DI-141 is in 141.txt Evidence Number "E4-f32" Alias "E4-f32" File "F:\E4-F32C.E01" was acquired by JRL at 08/30/02 10:07:07PM. The computer system clock read: 08/30/02 10:07:07PM. Evidence acquired under DOS 7.10 using version 3.20. The integrity of the following sector groups could not be verified:4096512-4096575 Drive Geometry: Total Size 2.9GB (6,152,832 sectors)

Case DI-141 for EnCase 3.20

	Volume "E4-f32" Parameters			
	File System:	FAT32	Drive Type:	Fixed
	Sectors Per Cluster:	4	Bytes Per Sector:	512
	Total Sectors:	6,152,832	Total Capacity:	3,137,974,272 bytes (2.9GB)
	Total Clusters:	1,532,214	Unallocated:	1,684,680,704 bytes (1.6GB)
	Free Clusters:	822,598	Allocated:	1,453,293,568 bytes (1.4GB)
	Volume Name:		Volume Offset:	0
	OEM Version:	MSWIN4.1	Volume Serial #:	0000-0000
	Heads:	255	Sectors Per Track:	63
	Unused Sectors:	63	Number of FATs:	2
	Sectors Per FAT:	11,972	Boot Sectors:	32

	EnCase Report Case: DI-141 Page = = = = Measurement Logs = = = = No compare log found for DI-141 Hash computed for this case (DI-141) Hash after test: 25BF8AF6B2D3E0BD1909C96E368DB27F51C49CBF
Expected Results:	Source disk is unchanged image verification error
Actual Results:	No anomalies
Analysis:	Expected results achieved

Case DI-142 for EnCase 3.20

Case Summary:	Create an image from an XBIOS-SCSI source disk to an XBIOS-SCSI destination disk and the source contains a FAT16 partition where the source disk is the same size as the destination
Tester Name:	JRL
Test Date:	Thu Sep 12 20:51:48 2002
PC:	HecRamsey
Disks:	Source: DOS Drive 80 Physical Label E3 Destination: DOS Drive 81 Physical Label 12 Image media: DOS Drive 80 Physical Label 7C E3 is a QUANTUM ATLAS10K2-TY092J with 17938985 sectors 12 is a FUJITSU MAN3184MC with 35885447 sectors 7C is a MAXTOR 6L040J2 with 78177792 sectors CD-ROM with PartitionMagic Pro 6.0 and boot floppy with run scripts FS-TST Release 1.0 CD-ROM + Baddisk 3.2 + Badx13 3.2
Source disk setup:	Dual boot Linux/Windows Me with EXT2 & Fat16 Disk: E3 Host: Cadfael Operator: JRL OS: Linux Red Hat 7.1/Windows Me Date: Sat Jul 21 16:17:29 2001 DISKWIPE.EXE E3_SRC Rumpole 80 E3 /src /new_log X:\pm\pqmagic /cmd=X:\pm\fat-src.txt Load Operating System to Source disk DISKHASH.EXE E3_SRC Rumpole 80 /before Disk hash = 0F9DACDA6C63D197C048782003D324108CEC7AB0
Destination Setup:	Z:\ss\DISKWIPE.EXE DI-142 HecRamsey 81 12 /noask /dst /new_log /comment JRL See CMPPTLOG.TXT for partition table
Error Setup:	none
Execute:	Z:\ss\DISKWIPE.EXE DI-142 HecRamsey 81 12 /noask /dst /new_log /comment JRL Z:\ss\PARTCMP.EXE DI-142 McCloud 80 E3 81 12 /new_log /comment JRL /select 1 1

Case DI-142 for EnCase 3.20	
	Z:\ss\DISKHASH.EXE DI-142 Wimsey 80 /comment E3(JRL) /new log /after
Log files loc:	test-archive/encase/encase-3.20/DI-142

Log File Highlights:	Source disk Drive 0x80, BIOS: Extensions Present
	Interrupt 13 bios 1022/254/63 (max cyl/hd values)
	Interrupt 13 ext 01023/255/63 (number of cyl/hd)
	17938985 total number of sectors reported via interrupt 13 from the BIOS
	<pre>N Start LBA Length Start C/H/S End C/H/S boot Partition type
	 1 P 000000063 001236942 0000/001/01 0076/254/63 Boot 06 Fat16
	 2 X 002249100 007181055 0140/000/01 0586/254/63 05 extended
	 3 S 000000063 000208782 0140/001/01 0152/254/63 83 Linux
	 4 x 000208845 000144585 0153/000/01 0161/254/63 05 extended
	 5 S 000000063 000144522 0153/001/01 0161/254/63 06 Fat16
	 6 x 004450005 000192780 0417/000/01 0428/254/63 05 extended
	 7 S 000000063 000192717 0417/001/01 0428/254/63 16 other
	 8 S 000000000 000000000 0000/000/00 0000/000/00 00 empty entry
	 9 P 009430155 006152895 0587/000/01 0969/254/63 83 Linux
	10 P 017510850 000417690 1023/000/01 1023/254/63 82 Linux swap</pre>Destination disk Drive 0x81, BIOS: Extensions Present
	Interrupt 13 bios 1022/254/63 (max cyl/hd values)
	Interrupt 13 ext 01023/255/63 (number of cyl/hd)
	35885448 total number of sectors reported via interrupt 13 from the BIOS
	<pre>N Start LBA Length Start C/H/S End C/H/S boot Partition type
	 1 P 000000063 001236942 0000/001/01 0076/254/63 06 Fat16
	 2 P 000000000 000000000 0000/000/00 0000/000/00 00 empty entry
	 3 P 000000000 000000000 0000/000/00 0000/000/00 00 empty entry
	 4 P 000000000 000000000 0000/000/00 0000/000/00 00 empty entry</pre>Image file acquired from DOS
	Restore environment Windows 2000
	EnCase report for case DI-142 is in 142.txt
	Evidence Number "E3-f16" Alias "E3-f16"
	
	File "G:\E3-F16.E01" was acquired by JRL at 09/12/02 08:55:09PM.
	The computer system clock read: 09/12/02 08:55:09PM.
	
	Evidence acquired under DOS 7.10 using version 3.20.
	
	File Integrity:
	Completely Verified, 0 Errors.
	Verification Hash: 1E23617EBDE0C9375EDA8F7A60CA62D9
	
	Drive Geometry:
	Total Size 604.0MB (1,236,942 sectors)
	
	Volume "E3-f16" Parameters

Volume "E3-f16" Parameters

File System:	FAT16	Drive Type:	Fixed
Sectors Per Cluster:	32	Bytes Per Sector:	512
Total Sectors:	1,236,942	Total Capacity:	633,126,912 bytes (603.8MB)
Total Clusters:	38,643	Unallocated:	85,213,184 bytes (81.3MB)
Free Clusters:	5,201	Allocated:	547,913,728 bytes (522.5MB)
Volume Name:		Volume Offset:	0
OEM Version:	MSWIN4.1	Volume Serial #:	3B65-7909
Heads:	255	Sectors Per Track:	63
Unused Sectors:	63	Number of FATs:	2
Sectors Per FAT:	151	Boot Sectors:	1

Case DI-142 for EnCase 3.20	
	EnCase Report Case: di-142 Page = = = = Measurement Logs = = = = Sectors Compared 1236942 Sectors Differ 0 Diffs range: Hash computed for this case (DI-142) Hash after test: 0F9DACDA6C63D197C048782003D324108CEC7AB0
Expected Results:	Source disk is unchanged src compares equal to dst
Actual Results:	No anomalies
Analysis:	Expected results achieved

Case DI-145 for EnCase 3.20	
Case Summary:	Create an image from an XBIOS-SCSI source disk to an XBIOS-SCSI destination disk and the source contains a FAT32 partition where the source disk is the same size as the destination Create the image on a removable medium. Introduce an error on the image.
Tester Name:	JRL
Test Date:	Fri Dec 06 11:55:12 2002
PC:	HecRamsey
Disks:	Source: DOS Drive 80 Physical Label E4 Destination: DOS Drive 81 Physical Label EB Image media: DOS Drive 80 Physical Label 7C E4 is a QUANTUM ATLAS10K2-TY092J with 17938985 sectors EB is a SEAGATE ST39204LC with 17921835 sectors 7C is a MAXTOR 6L040J2 with 78177792 sectors CD-ROM with PartitionMagic Pro 6.0 and boot floppy with run scripts FS-TST Release 1.0 CD-ROM + Baddisk 3.2 + Badx13 3.2
Source disk setup:	Windows 2000 with NTFS & Fat32 Disk: E4 Host: JudgeDee Operator: JRL OS: Windows 2000/NT Date: Sat Jul 21 16:58:28 2001 DISKWIPE.EXE E4_SRC JudgeDee 80 E4 /src /noask /comment Windows 2000 source disk X:\pm\pqmagic /cmd=X:\pm\nt-src.txt Load Operating System to Source disk cmd: X:\ss\DISKHASH.EXE Hash Wimsey 80 /comment E4 /new_log /before Disk hash = 25BF8AF6B2D3E0BD1909C96E368DB27F51C49CBF
Destination Setup:	Z:\ss\DISKWIPE.EXE DI-145 HecRamsey 81 EB /noask /dst /new_log /comment JRL See CMPPTLOG.TXT for partition table
Error Setup:	cmd: Z:\ss\CORRUPT.EXE DI-145 HecRamsey D:\e4-ft32.e02 656147 5A Comment: Change 255/001/01 to 255/Z01/01 at LBA 4096638
Execute:	Z:\ss\DISKWIPE.EXE DI-145 HecRamsey 81 EB /noask /dst /new_log /comment JRL Z:\ss\PARTCMP.EXE DI-145 JudgeDee 80 E4 81 EB /new_log /comment JRL /select 1 1 Z:\ss\DISKHASH.EXE DI-145 JudgeDee 80 /comment E4(JRL) /new_log /after
Log files loc:	test-archive/encase/encase-3.20/DI-145

Log File Highlights:	Source disk Drive 0x80, BIOS: Extensions Present
	Interrupt 13 bios 1022/254/63 (max cyl/hd values)
	Interrupt 13 ext 01023/255/63 (number of cyl/hd)
	17938985 total number of sectors reported via interrupt 13 from the
	BIOS
	<pre>N Start LBA Length Start C/H/S End C/H/S boot Partition type
	1 P 000000063 006152832 0000/001/01 0382/254/63 Boot 0B Fat32
	2 X 008193150 009735390 0510/000/01 1023/254/63 0F extended
	3 S 000000000 000000000 0000/000/00 0000/000/00 00 empty entry
	4 x 002056320 001237005 0638/000/01 0714/254/63 05 extended
	5 S 000000063 001236942 0638/001/01 0714/254/63 07 NTFS
	6 x 005349645 001638630 0843/000/01 0944/254/63 05 extended
	7 S 000000063 001638567 0843/001/01 0944/254/63 17 other
	8 x 008498385 001237005 1023/000/01 1023/254/63 05 extended
	9 S 000000063 001236942 1023/001/01 1023/254/63 1B other</pre>

Case DI-145 for EnCase 3.20

```
10 S 000000000 000000000 0000/000/00 0000/000/00        00 empty entry
11 P 000000000 000000000 0000/000/00 0000/000/00        00 empty entry
12 P 000000000 000000000 0000/000/00 0000/000/00        00 empty entry
Destination disk Drive 0x81, BIOS: Extensions Present
Interrupt 13  bios  1022/254/63 (max cyl/hd values)
Interrupt 13  ext  01023/255/63 (number of cyl/hd)
17921835 total number of sectors reported via interrupt 13 from the
BIOS
 N   Start LBA Length    Start C/H/S End C/H/S   boot Partition type
 1 P 000000063 006152832 0000/001/01 0382/254/63      0B Fat32
 2 P 000000000 000000000 0000/000/00 0000/000/00      00 empty entry
 3 P 000000000 000000000 0000/000/00 0000/000/00      00 empty entry
 4 P 000000000 000000000 0000/000/00 0000/000/00      00 empty entry
Image file acquired from DOS
Restore environment Windows 2000
EnCase report for case DI-145 is in 145.txt
Evidence Number "E4-f32"   Alias "E4-f32"

File "D:\E4-FT32.E01" was acquired by JRL at 12/06/02 12:15:01PM.
The computer system clock read: 12/06/02 12:15:01PM.

Evidence acquired under DOS 7.10 using version 3.20.

The integrity of the following sector groups could not be
verified:4096512-4096575
Drive Geometry:
Total Size     2.9GB (6,152,832 sectors)
```

Volume "E4-f32" Parameters

File System:	FAT32	Drive Type:	Fixed
Sectors Per Cluster:	4	Bytes Per Sector:	512
Total Sectors:	6,152,832	Total Capacity:	3,137,974,272 bytes (2.9GB)
Total Clusters:	1,532,214	Unallocated:	1,684,680,704 bytes (1.6GB)
Free Clusters:	822,598	Allocated:	1,453,293,568 bytes (1.4GB)
Volume Name:		Volume Offset:	0
OEM Version:	MSWIN4.1	Volume Serial #:	0000-0000
Heads:	255	Sectors Per Track:	63
Unused Sectors:	63	Number of FATs:	2
Sectors Per FAT:	11,972	Boot Sectors:	32

```
EnCase Report
Case: DI-145   Page

= = = = Measurement Logs = = = =
Sectors Compared 6152832
Sectors Differ 1
Diffs range:  4096575
Hash computed for this case (DI-145)
Hash after test: 25BF8AF6B2D3E0BD1909C96E368DB27F51C49CBF
```

Expected Results:	Source disk is unchanged image verification error
Actual Results:	No anomalies
Analysis:	Expected results achieved

Case DI-147 for EnCase 3.20

Case Summary:	Create an image from an XBIOS-SCSI source disk to an XBIOS-SCSI destination disk and the source contains a FAT32 partition where the source disk is larger than the destination
Tester Name:	JRL

Case DI-147 for EnCase 3.20	
Test Date:	Fri Jun 14 09:37:58 2002
PC:	Wimsey
Disks:	Source: DOS Drive 80 Physical Label E4 Destination: DOS Drive 81 Physical Label 11 Image media: DOS Drive 80 Physical Label 7C E4 is a QUANTUM ATLAS10K2-TY092J with 17938985 sectors 11 is a FUJITSU MAN3184MC with 35885447 sectors 7C is a MAXTOR 6L040J2 with 78177792 sectors CD-ROM with PartitionMagic Pro 6.0 and boot floppy with run scripts FS-TST Release 1.0 CD-ROM + Baddisk 3.2 + Badx13 3.2
Source disk setup:	Windows 2000 with NTFS & Fat32 Disk: E4 Host: JudgeDee Operator: JRL OS: Windows 2000/NT Date: Sat Jul 21 16:58:28 2001 DISKWIPE.EXE E4_SRC JudgeDee 80 E4 /src /noask /comment Windows 2000 source disk X:\pm\pqmagic /cmd=X:\pm\nt-src.txt Load Operating System to Source disk cmd: X:\ss\DISKHASH.EXE Hash Wimsey 80 /comment E4 /new_log /before Disk hash = 25BF8AF6B2D3E0BD1909C96E368DB27F51C49CBF
Destination Setup:	Z:\ss\DISKWIPE.EXE DI-147 Wimsey 81 11 /noask /dst /new_log /comment JRL See CMPPTLOG.TXT for partition table
Error Setup:	none
Execute:	Z:\ss\DISKWIPE.EXE DI-147 Wimsey 81 11 /noask /dst /new_log /comment JRL Z:\ss\PARTCMP.EXE DI-147 Wimsey 80 E4 81 11 /new_log /comment JRL /select 1 1
Log files loc:	test-archive/encase/encase-3.20/DI-147

Log File Highlights:	Source disk Drive 0x80, BIOS: Extensions Present
	Interrupt 13 bios 1022/254/63 (max cyl/hd values)
	Interrupt 13 ext 01023/255/63 (number of cyl/hd)
	17938985 total number of sectors reported via interrupt 13 from the
	BIOS
	<pre>N Start LBA Length Start C/H/S End C/H/S boot Partition type
	 1 P 000000063 006152832 0000/001/01 0382/254/63 Boot 0B Fat32
	 2 X 008193150 009735390 0510/000/01 1023/254/63 0F extended
	 3 S 000000000 000000000 0000/000/00 0000/000/00 00 empty entry
	 4 x 002056320 001237005 0638/000/01 0714/254/63 05 extended
	 5 S 000000063 001236942 0638/001/01 0714/254/63 07 NTFS
	 6 x 005349645 001638630 0843/000/01 0944/254/63 05 extended
	 7 S 000000063 001638567 0843/001/01 0944/254/63 17 other
	 8 x 008498385 001237005 1023/000/01 1023/254/63 05 extended
	 9 S 000000063 001236942 1023/001/01 1023/254/63 1B other
	10 S 000000000 000000000 0000/000/00 0000/000/00 00 empty entry
	11 P 000000000 000000000 0000/000/00 0000/000/00 00 empty entry
	12 P 000000000 000000000 0000/000/00 0000/000/00 00 empty entry</pre>Destination disk Drive 0x81, BIOS: Extensions Present
	Interrupt 13 bios 1022/254/63 (max cyl/hd values)
	Interrupt 13 ext 01023/255/63 (number of cyl/hd)
	35885448 total number of sectors reported via interrupt 13 from the
	BIOS
	<pre>N Start LBA Length Start C/H/S End C/H/S boot Partition type
	 1 P 000000063 005943987 0000/001/01 0369/254/63 0B Fat32
	 2 P 000000000 000000000 0000/000/00 0000/000/00 00 empty entry
	 3 P 000000000 000000000 0000/000/00 0000/000/00 00 empty entry
	 4 P 000000000 000000000 0000/000/00 0000/000/00 00 empty entry</pre>Image file acquired from DOS
	Restore environment Windows 2000
	EnCase report for case DI-147 is in E4-fat32.txt
	Evidence Number "1" Alias "1"
	
	File "D:\E4-FAT32.E01" was acquired by JRL at 06/11/02 04:50:21PM.
	The computer system clock read: 06/11/02 04:50:21PM.
	
	Evidence acquired under DOS 7.10 using version 3.20.
	
	File Integrity:
	Completely Verified, 0 Errors.

Verification Hash: 25B37B7DFDDFACB085841B6686FA642E

Drive Geometry:
Total Size   2.9GB (6,152,832 sectors)

Volume "1" Parameters

File System:	FAT32	Drive Type:	Fixed
Sectors Per Cluster:	4	Bytes Per Sector:	512
Total Sectors:	6,152,832	Total Capacity:	3,137,974,272 bytes (2.9GB)
Total Clusters:	1,532,214	Unallocated:	1,684,680,704 bytes (1.6GB)
Free Clusters:	822,598	Allocated:	1,453,293,568 bytes (1.4GB)
Volume Name:		Volume Offset:	0
OEM Version:	MSWIN4.1	Volume Serial #:	0000-0000
Heads:	255	Sectors Per Track:	63
Unused Sectors:	63	Number of FATs:	2
Sectors Per FAT:	11,972	Boot Sectors:	32

EnCase Report
Case: E4-FAT32 Page

= = = = Measurement Logs = = = =
Sectors Compared 5943987
Sectors Differ 1
Diffs range: 1
Source (6152832) has 208845 more sectors than destination (5943987)
This case uses the hash computed from case DI-130
Hash after test: 25BF8AF6B2D3E0BD1909C96E368DB27F51C49CBF

Expected Results:	Source disk is unchanged src compares qualified equal to dst, src is truncated on dst truncation is logged
Actual Results:	Logical restore anomaly
Analysis:	Expected results not achieved

Case Summary:	Create an image from a direct access IDE source disk to a direct access IDE destination disk where the source disk is smaller than the destination Introduce an error on the image.
Tester Name:	JRL
Test Date:	Tue Sep 03 12:45:58 2002
PC:	Beta3
Disks:	Source: DOS Drive 80 Physical Label F1 Destination: DOS Drive 81 Physical Label none Image media: DOS Drive 80 Physical Label D3 F1 is a Quantum Sirooco1700A with 3335472 sectors D3 is a Fujitsu MPE3064AT with 12672450 sectors CD-ROM with PartitionMagic Pro 6.0 and boot floppy with run scripts FS-TST Release 1.0 CD-ROM + Baddisk 3.2 + Badx13 3.2
Source disk setup:	Linux EXT2 & Fat32 Disk: F1 Host: JudgeDee Operator: JRL OS: Windows/Me Options: Typical Date: Fri Nov 16 10:42:33 2001 cmd: Z:\ss\DISKWIPE.EXE F1 JudgeDee 80 F1 /src /new_log X:\pm\pqmagic /cmd=X:\pm\f32-src.txt Load Operating System to Source disk

Case DI-149 for EnCase 3.20

	cmd: Z:\ss\DISKHASH.EXE F1 JudgeDee 80 /before /new_log Disk hash = 3E7E5E0AB0FA333BE39D267F0DB8E340386DC05A
Destination Setup:	No destination setup required
Error Setup:	cmd: Z:\ss\CORRUPT.EXE DI-149 Beta3 D:\f1-ata.e01 476220610 41 Comment: Change 923/001/01 to 923/00A/01 at LBA 930447
Execute:	Z:\ss\DISKHASH.EXE DI-149 JudgeDee 80 /comment F1(JRL) /new_log /after
Log files loc:	test-archive/encase/encase-3.20/DI-149
Log File Highlights:	Image file acquired from DOS Restore environment Windows 98 EnCase report for case DI-149 is in 149.txt Evidence Number "F1-All" Alias "F1-All" File "D:\F1-ata.e01" was acquired by JRL at 09/03/02 12:48:53PM. The computer system clock read: 09/03/02 12:48:53PM. Evidence acquired under DOS 7.10 using version 3.20. The integrity of the following sector groups could not be verified:930432-930495 Drive Geometry: Total Size 1.6GB (3,335,472 sectors) Cylinders: 3,309 Heads: 16 Sectors: 63 Partitions: <table><tr><td>Code</td><td>Type</td><td>Start Sector</td><td>Total Sectors</td><td>Size</td></tr><tr><td>0B</td><td>FAT32</td><td>0</td><td>1229760</td><td>600.5MB</td></tr><tr><td>83</td><td>Linux EXT2</td><td>2721600</td><td>64512</td><td>31.5MB</td></tr><tr><td>82</td><td>Linux Swap</td><td>2923200</td><td>411264</td><td>200.8MB</td></tr><tr><td>83</td><td>Linux EXT2</td><td>1431360</td><td>205632</td><td>100.4MB</td></tr><tr><td>0B</td><td>FAT32</td><td>1636992</td><td>145152</td><td>70.9MB</td></tr><tr><td>16</td><td>HiddenFAT16</td><td>2193408</td><td>185472</td><td>90.6MB</td></tr></table> EnCase Report Case: DI-149 Page = = = = Measurement Logs = = = = No compare log found for DI-149 Hash computed for this case (DI-149) Hash after test: 3E7E5E0AB0FA333BE39D267F0DB8E340386DC05A
Expected Results:	Source disk is unchanged image verification error
Actual Results:	No anomalies
Analysis:	Expected results achieved

Case DI-150 for EnCase 3.20

Case Summary:	Create an image from a direct access IDE source disk to a direct access IDE destination disk where the source disk is smaller than the destination
Tester Name:	JRL
Test Date:	Thu Jun 06 08:15:13 2002
PC:	Cadfael
Disks:	Source: DOS Drive 80 Physical Label F5 Destination: DOS Drive 81 Physical Label 93 Image media: DOS Drive 80 Physical Label 7C F5 is an IBM-DTLA-307020 with 40188960 sectors 93 is a WDC WD300BB-00CAA0 with 58633344 sectors 7C is a MAXTOR 6L040J2 with 78177792 sectors CD-ROM with PartitionMagic Pro 6.0 and boot floppy with run scripts FS-TST Release 1.0 CD-ROM + Baddisk 3.2 + Badx13 3.2
Source disk setup:	Dual boot Linux/Windows Me with EXT2 & Fat16 Disk: F5 Host: Cadfael

Case DI-150 for EnCase 3.20	
	Operator: JRL OS: WindowsMe/Linux Date: Sat Aug 11 11:13:43 2001 DISKWIPE.EXE F5_SRC Cadfael 80 F5 /src X:\pm\pqmagic /cmd=X:\pm\fat-src.txt Load Operating System to Source disk DISKHASH.EXE F5_SRC Cadfael 80 /before Disk hash = 83A0002816BBF089F8BE33C41C92C3B5A0F42A54
Destination Setup:	Z:\ss\DISKWIPE.EXE DI-150 Cadfael 81 93 /noask /dst /new_log /comment JRL No partition table defined
Error Setup:	none
Execute:	Z:\ss\DISKWIPE.EXE DI-150 Cadfael 81 93 /noask /dst /new_log /comment JRL Z:\ss\DISKCMP.EXE DI-150 Cadfael 80 F5 81 93 /new_log /comment JRL
Log files loc:	test-archive/encase/encase-3.20/DI-150
Log File Highlights:	Image file acquired from DOS Restore environment Windows 2000 EnCase report for case DI-150 is in F5-ATA.txt Evidence Number "F5-ATA-1" Alias "F5-ATA-1" File "D:\F5-ATA.E01" was acquired by JRL at 06/03/02 02:54:01PM. The computer system clock read: 06/03/02 02:54:01PM. Evidence acquired under DOS 7.10 using version 3.20. File Integrity: Completely Verified, 0 Errors. Verification Hash: 849BAEFDE9407109B9D22FBB479FE00D Drive Geometry: Total Size 19.2GB (40,188,960 sectors) Cylinders: 16,383 Heads: 16 Sectors: 63 Partitions: | Code	Type	Start Sector	Total Sectors	Size
---	---	---	---	---
06	BIGDOS	0	1237005	604.0MB
83	Linux EXT2	9430155	6152895	2.9GB
82	Linux Swap	39760875	417690	204.0MB
83	Linux EXT2	2249100	208845	102.0MB
06	BIGDOS	2457945	144585	70.6MB
16	HiddenFAT16	6699105	192780	94.1MB	 EnCase Report Case: F5-ata Page = = = = Measurement Logs = = = = Sectors Compared 40188960 Sectors Differ 0 Diffs range Source (40188960) has 18444384 fewer sectors than destination (58633344) Zero fill: 0 Src Byte fill (F5): 0 Dst Byte fill (93): 18444384 Other fill: 0 Other no fill: 0 This case uses the hash computed from case DI-153 Hash after test: 83A0002816BBF089F8BE33C41C92C3B5A0F42A54
Expected Results:	Source disk is unchanged src compares qualified equal to dst
Actual Results:	No anomalies

Case DI-150 for EnCase 3.20	
Analysis:	Expected results achieved

Case DI-152 for EnCase 3.20	
Case Summary:	Create an image from a direct access IDE source disk to a direct access IDE destination disk where the source disk is the same size as the destination
Tester Name:	JRL
Test Date:	Thu Jun 06 07:17:17 2002
PC:	Rumpole
Disks:	Source: DOS Drive 80 Physical Label F5 Destination: DOS Drive 81 Physical Label F7 Image media: DOS Drive 80 Physical Label 7C F5 is an IBM-DTLA-307020 with 40188960 sectors F7 is an IBM-DTLA-307020 with 40188960 sectors 7C is a MAXTOR 6L040J2 with 78177792 sectors CD-ROM with PartitionMagic Pro 6.0 and boot floppy with run scripts FS-TST Release 1.0 CD-ROM + Baddisk 3.2 + Badx13 3.2
Source disk setup:	Dual boot Linux/Windows Me with EXT2 & Fat16 Disk: F5 Host: Cadfael Operator: JRL OS: WindowsMe/Linux Date: Sat Aug 11 11:13:43 2001 DISKWIPE.EXE F5_SRC Cadfael 80 F5 /src X:\pm\pqmagic /cmd=X:\pm\fat-src.txt Load Operating System to Source disk DISKHASH.EXE F5_SRC Cadfael 80 /before Disk hash = 83A0002816BBF089F8BE33C41C92C3B5A0F42A54
Destination Setup:	Z:\ss\DISKWIPE.EXE DI-152 Rumpole 81 F7 /noask /dst /new_log /comment JRL No partition table defined
Error Setup:	none
Execute:	Z:\ss\DISKWIPE.EXE DI-152 Rumpole 81 F7 /noask /dst /new_log /comment JRL Z:\ss\DISKCMP.EXE DI-152 Cadfael 80 F5 81 F7 /new_log /comment JRL
Log files loc:	test-archive/encase/encase-3.20/DI-152
Log File Highlights:	Image file acquired from DOS Restore environment Windows 2000 EnCase report for case DI-152 is in F5-ATA.txt Evidence Number "F5-ATA-1" Alias "F5-ATA-1" File "D:\F5-ATA.E01" was acquired by JRL at 06/03/02 02:54:01PM. The computer system clock read: 06/03/02 02:54:01PM. Evidence acquired under DOS 7.10 using version 3.20. File Integrity: Completely Verified, 0 Errors. Verification Hash: 849BAEFDE9407109B9D22FBB479FE00D Drive Geometry: Total Size 19.2GB (40,188,960 sectors) Cylinders: 16,383 Heads: 16 Sectors: 63

Partitions:

Code	Type	Start Sector	Total Sectors	Size
06	BIGDOS	0	1237005	604.0MB
83	Linux EXT2	9430155	6152895	2.9GB
82	Linux Swap	39760875	417690	204.0MB
83	Linux EXT2	2249100	208845	102.0MB
06	BIGDOS	2457945	144585	70.6MB
16	HiddenFAT16	6699105	192780	94.1MB

Case DI-152 for EnCase 3.20	
	EnCase Report Case: F5-ata Page = = = = Measurement Logs = = = = Sectors Compared 40188960 Sectors Differ 10395 Diffs range 40178565-40188959 This case uses the hash computed from case DI-153 Hash after test: 83A0002816BBF089F8BE33C41C92C3B5A0F42A54
Expected Results:	Source disk is unchanged src compares equal to dst
Actual Results:	Restore anomaly
Analysis:	Expected results not achieved

Case DI-153 for EnCase 3.20	
Case Summary:	Create an image from a direct access IDE source disk to a direct access IDE destination disk where the source disk is larger than the destination
Tester Name:	JRL
Test Date:	Thu Jun 06 08:26:09 2002
PC:	Wimsey
Disks:	Source: DOS Drive 80 Physical Label F5 Destination: DOS Drive 81 Physical Label A6 Image media: DOS Drive 80 Physical Label 7C F5 is an IBM-DTLA-307020 with 40188960 sectors A6 is a WDC WD200BB-00AUA1 with 39102336 sectors 7C is a MAXTOR 6L040J2 with 78177792 sectors CD-ROM with PartitionMagic Pro 6.0 and boot floppy with run scripts FS-TST Release 1.0 CD-ROM + Baddisk 3.2 + Badx13 3.2
Source disk setup:	Dual boot Linux/Windows Me with EXT2 & Fat16 Disk: F5 Host: Cadfael Operator: JRL OS: WindowsMe/Linux Date: Sat Aug 11 11:13:43 2001 DISKWIPE.EXE F5_SRC Cadfael 80 F5 /src X:\pm\pqmagic /cmd=X:\pm\fat-src.txt Load Operating System to Source disk DISKHASH.EXE F5_SRC Cadfael 80 /before Disk hash = 83A0002816BBF089F8BE33C41C92C3B5A0F42A54
Destination Setup:	Z:\ss\DISKWIPE.EXE DI-153 Wimsey 81 A6 /noask /dst /new_log /comment JRL No partition table defined
Error Setup:	none
Execute:	Z:\ss\DISKWIPE.EXE DI-153 Wimsey 81 A6 /noask /dst /new_log /comment JRL Z:\ss\DISKCMP.EXE DI-153 Wimsey 80 F5 81 A6 /new_log /comment JRL Z:\ss\DISKHASH.EXE DI-153 Wimsey 80 /comment F5(JRL) /new_log /after
Log files loc:	test-archive/encase/encase-3.20/DI-153
Log File Highlights:	Image file acquired from DOS Restore environment Windows 2000 EnCase report for case DI-153 is in F5-ATA.txt Evidence Number "F5-ATA-1" Alias "F5-ATA-1" File "D:\F5-ATA.E01" was acquired by JRL at 06/03/02 02:54:01PM. The computer system clock read: 06/03/02 02:54:01PM. Evidence acquired under DOS 7.10 using version 3.20. File Integrity: Completely Verified, 0 Errors. Verification Hash: 849BAEFDE9407109B9D22FBB479FE00D Drive Geometry: Total Size 19.2GB (40,188,960 sectors) Cylinders: 16,383 Heads: 16 Sectors: 63

Case DI-153 for EnCase 3.20

Partitions:

Code	Type	Start Sector	Total Sectors	Size
06	BIGDOS	0	1237005	604.0MB
83	Linux EXT2	9430155	6152895	2.9GB
82	Linux Swap	39760875	417690	204.0MB
83	Linux EXT2	2249100	208845	102.0MB
06	BIGDOS	2457945	144585	70.6MB
16	HiddenFAT16	6699105	192780	94.1MB

EnCase Report
Case: F5-ata   Page

= = = = Measurement Logs = = = =
Sectors Compared 39102336
Sectors Differ 126
Diffs range 39102210-39102335
Source (40188960) has 1086624 more sectors than destination (39102336)
Hash computed for this case (DI-153)
Hash after test: 83A0002816BBF089F8BE33C41C92C3B5A0F42A54

Expected Results:	Source disk is unchanged src compares qualified equal to dst, src is truncated on dst truncation is logged
Actual Results:	Restore anomaly
Analysis:	Expected results not achieved

Case DI-154 for EnCase 3.20

Case Summary:	Create an image from an ASPI SCSI source disk to an ASPI SCSI destination disk where the source disk is smaller than the destination Introduce an error on the image.
Tester Name:	JRL
Test Date:	Fri Dec 06 22:07:39 2002
PC:	McCloud
Disks:	Source: DOS Drive 80 Physical Label E3 Destination: DOS Drive 81 Physical Label E6 Image media: DOS Drive 80 Physical Label 91 E3 is a QUANTUM ATLAS10K2-TY092J with 17938985 sectors E6 is a SEAGATE ST318404LC with 35843670 sectors 91 is a WDC WD300BB-00CAA0 with 58633344 sectors CD-ROM with PartitionMagic Pro 6.0 and boot floppy with run scripts FS-TST Release 1.0 CD-ROM + Baddisk 3.2 + Badx13 3.2
Source disk setup:	Dual boot Linux/Windows Me with EXT2 & Fat16 Disk: E3 Host: Cadfael Operator: JRL OS: Linux Red Hat 7.1/Windows Me Date: Sat Jul 21 16:17:29 2001 DISKWIPE.EXE E3_SRC Rumpole 80 E3 /src /new_log X:\pm\pqmagic /cmd=X:\pm\fat-src.txt Load Operating System to Source disk DISKHASH.EXE E3_SRC Rumpole 80 /before Disk hash = 0F9DACDA6C63D197C048782003D324108CEC7AB0
Destination Setup:	Z:\ss\DISKWIPE.EXE DI-154 McCloud 81 E6 /noask /dst /new_log /comment JRL No partition table defined
Error Setup:	cmd: Z:\ss\CORRUPT.EXE DI-154 McCloud D:\E3.e02 1044805 51 Comment: Change 255/009/01 to 255/00Q/01 at LBA 4097142
Execute:	Z:\ss\DISKWIPE.EXE DI-154 McCloud 81 E6 /noask /dst /new_log /comment JRL Z:\ss\DISKCMP.EXE DI-154 Wimsey 80 E3 81 E6 /new_log /comment JRL Z:\ss\DISKHASH.EXE DI-154 Wimsey 80 /comment E3(JRL) /new_log /after
Log files loc:	test-archive/encase/encase-3.20/DI-154
Log File	Image file acquired from DOS

Case DI-154 for EnCase 3.20

Highlights:	Restore environment Windows 98 EnCase report for case DI-154 is in 154.txt Evidence Number "E3-all" Alias "E3-all" File "D:\E3.e01" was acquired by JRL at 12/07/02 02:07:22AM. The computer system clock read: 12/07/02 02:07:22AM. Evidence acquired under DOS 7.10 using version 3.20. The integrity of the following sector groups could not be verified:4097088-4097151 Drive Geometry: Total Size 8.6GB (17,938,985 sectors)

Partitions:

Code	Type	Start Sector	Total Sectors	Size
06	BIGDOS	0	1237005	604.0MB
83	Linux EXT2	9430155	6152895	2.9GB
82	Linux Swap	17510850	417690	204.0MB
83	Linux EXT2	2249100	208845	102.0MB
06	BIGDOS	2457945	144585	70.6MB
16	HiddenFAT16	6699105	192780	94.1MB

```
EnCase Report
Case: DI-154    Page

= = = = Measurement Logs = = = =
Sectors Compared 17938985
Sectors Differ 1
Diffs range 4097142
Source (17938985) has 17904685 fewer sectors than destination
(35843670)
Zero fill:          17904685
Src Byte fill (E3):        0
Dst Byte fill (E6):        0
Other fill:               0
Other no fill:            0
Hash computed for this case (DI-154)
Hash after test: 0F9DACDA6C63D197C048782003D324108CEC7AB0
```

Expected Results:	Source disk is unchanged image verification error
Actual Results:	No anomalies
Analysis:	Expected results achieved

Case DI-160 for EnCase 3.20

Case Summary:	Create an image from an XBIOS-IDE source disk to an XBIOS-SCSI destination disk where the source disk is smaller than the destination
Tester Name:	JRL
Test Date:	Thu Jun 06 09:10:05 2002
PC:	AndWife
Disks:	Source: DOS Drive 80 Physical Label 94 Destination: DOS Drive 81 Physical Label CC Image media: DOS Drive 80 Physical Label 75 94 is a WDC WD300BB-00CAA0 with 58633344 sectors CC is a SEAGATE ST336705LC with 71687370 sectors 75 is a IC35L040AVER07-0 with 80418240 sectors CD-ROM with PartitionMagic Pro 6.0 and boot floppy with run scripts FS-TST Release 1.0 CD-ROM + Baddisk 3.2 + Badx13 3.2
Source disk setup:	Linux EXT2 & Fat32 Disk: 94 Host: McMillan Operator: JRL OS: Windows/Me Options: Typical

Case DI-160 for EnCase 3.20	
	Date: Tue Jun 04 01:59:45 2002 cmd: Z:\ss\DISKWIPE.EXE 94 McMillan 80 94 /src /new_log X:\pm\pqmagic /cmd=X:\pm\f32-src.txt Load Operating System to Source disk cmd: Z:\ss\DISKHASH.EXE 94 McMillan 80 /before /new_log Disk hash = FA03D9CA7ECD0D7CED83FBC05FD74465761020B9
Destination Setup:	Z:\ss\DISKWIPE.EXE DI-160 AndWife 81 CC /noask /dst /new_log /comment JRL No partition table defined
Error Setup:	none
Execute:	Z:\ss\DISKWIPE.EXE DI-160 AndWife 81 CC /noask /dst /new_log /comment JRL Z:\ss\DISKCMP.EXE DI-160 McCloud 80 94 81 CC /new_log /comment JRL
Log files loc:	test-archive/encase/encase-3.20/DI-160
Log File Highlights:	Image file acquired from DOS Restore environment Windows 2000 EnCase report for case DI-160 is in 94.txt Evidence Number "94" Alias "94" File "D:\94.E01" was acquired by JRL at 06/06/02 08:46:27PM. The computer system clock read: 06/06/02 08:46:27PM. Evidence acquired under DOS 7.10 using version 3.20. File Integrity: Completely Verified, 0 Errors. Verification Hash: 211FEC4CA99418D8068D0369643E6B80 Drive Geometry: Total Size 28.0GB (58,633,344 sectors) Cylinders: 16,383 Heads: 16 Sectors: 63 Partitions:<table><tr><td>Code</td><td>Type</td><td>Start Sector</td><td>Total Sectors</td><td>Size</td></tr><tr><td>0B</td><td>FAT32</td><td>0</td><td>1237005</td><td>604.0MB</td></tr><tr><td>83</td><td>Linux EXT2</td><td>58010715</td><td>64260</td><td>31.4MB</td></tr><tr><td>82</td><td>Linux Swap</td><td>58203495</td><td>417690</td><td>204.0MB</td></tr><tr><td>83</td><td>Linux EXT2</td><td>1429785</td><td>208845</td><td>102.0MB</td></tr><tr><td>0B</td><td>FAT32</td><td>1638630</td><td>144585</td><td>70.6MB</td></tr><tr><td>16</td><td>HiddenFAT16</td><td>2200905</td><td>192780</td><td>94.1MB</td></tr></table> EnCase Report Case: 94 Page = = = = Measurement Logs = = = = Sectors Compared 58633344 Sectors Differ 0 Diffs range Source (58633344) has 13054026 fewer sectors than destination (71687370) Zero fill: 0 Src Byte fill (94): 0 Dst Byte fill (CC): 13054026 Other fill: 0 Other no fill: 0 This case uses the hash computed from case DI-161 Hash after test: FA03D9CA7ECD0D7CED83FBC05FD74465761020B9
Expected Results:	Source disk is unchanged src compares qualified equal to dst
Actual Results:	No anomalies
Analysis:	Expected results achieved

Case DI-161 for EnCase 3.20	
Case Summary:	Create an image from an XBIOS-IDE source disk to an XBIOS-SCSI destination disk where the source disk is larger than the destination
Tester Name:	JRL
Test Date:	Thu Jun 06 21:20:06 2002
PC:	McCloud
Disks:	Source: DOS Drive 80 Physical Label 94 Destination: DOS Drive 81 Physical Label 1F Image media: DOS Drive 80 Physical Label 75 94 is a WDC WD300BB-00CAA0 with 58633344 sectors 1F is a QUANTUM ATLAS10K3_18_SCA with 35916547 sectors 75 is a IC35L040AVER07-0 with 80418240 sectors CD-ROM with PartitionMagic Pro 6.0 and boot floppy with run scripts FS-TST Release 1.0 CD-ROM + Baddisk 3.2 + Badx13 3.2
Source disk setup:	Linux EXT2 & Fat32 Disk: 94 Host: McMillan Operator: JRL OS: Windows/Me Options: Typical Date: Tue Jun 04 01:59:45 2002 cmd: Z:\ss\DISKWIPE.EXE 94 McMillan 80 94 /src /new_log X:\pm\pqmagic /cmd=X:\pm\f32-src.txt Load Operating System to Source disk cmd: Z:\ss\DISKHASH.EXE 94 McMillan 80 /before /new_log Disk hash = FA03D9CA7ECD0D7CED83FBC05FD74465761020B9
Destination Setup:	Z:\ss\DISKWIPE.EXE DI-161 McCloud 81 1F /noask /dst /new_log /comment JRL No partition table defined
Error Setup:	none
Execute:	Z:\ss\DISKWIPE.EXE DI-161 McCloud 81 1F /noask /dst /new_log /comment JRL Z:\ss\DISKCMP.EXE DI-161 McCloud 80 94 81 1F /new_log /comment JRL Z:\ss\DISKHASH.EXE DI-161 McCloud 80 /comment 94(JRL) /new_log /after
Log files loc:	test-archive/encase/encase-3.20/DI-161
Log File Highlights:	Image file acquired from DOS Restore environment Windows 2000 EnCase report for case DI-161 is in 94.txt Evidence Number "94" Alias "94" File "D:\94.E01" was acquired by JRL at 06/06/02 08:46:27PM. The computer system clock read: 06/06/02 08:46:27PM. Evidence acquired under DOS 7.10 using version 3.20. File Integrity: Completely Verified, 0 Errors. Verification Hash: 211FEC4CA99418D8068D0369643E6B80 Drive Geometry: Total Size 28.0GB (58,633,344 sectors) Cylinders: 16,383 Heads: 16 Sectors: 63 Partitions:

Code	Type	Start Sector	Total Sectors	Size
0B	FAT32	0	1237005	604.0MB
83	Linux EXT2	58010715	64260	31.4MB
82	Linux Swap	58203495	417690	204.0MB
83	Linux EXT2	1429785	208845	102.0MB
0B	FAT32	1638630	144585	70.6MB
16	HiddenFAT16	2200905	192780	94.1MB

Case DI-161 for EnCase 3.20

	EnCase Report Case: 94 Page = = = = Measurement Logs = = = = Sectors Compared 35916548 Sectors Differ 11273 Diffs range 35905275-35916547 Source (58633344) has 22716796 more sectors than destination (35916548) Hash computed for this case (DI-161) Hash after test: FA03D9CA7ECD0D7CED83FBC05FD74465761020B9
Expected Results:	Source disk is unchanged src compares qualified equal to dst, src is truncated on dst truncation is logged
Actual Results:	Restore anomaly
Analysis:	Expected results not achieved

Case DI-163 for EnCase 3.20

Case Summary:	Create an image from an XBIOS-SCSI source disk to an XBIOS-IDE destination disk where the source disk is smaller than the destination
Tester Name:	JRL
Test Date:	Fri Jun 07 14:06:39 2002
PC:	AndWife
Disks:	Source: DOS Drive 80 Physical Label E4 Destination: DOS Drive 81 Physical Label 9F Image media: DOS Drive 80 Physical Label 7C E4 is a QUANTUM ATLAS10K2-TY092J with 17938985 sectors 9F is a WDC WD200BB-32CFC0 with 39102336 sectors 7C is a MAXTOR 6L040J2 with 78177792 sectors CD-ROM with PartitionMagic Pro 6.0 and boot floppy with run scripts FS-TST Release 1.0 CD-ROM + Baddisk 3.2 + Badx13 3.2
Source disk setup:	Windows 2000 with NTFS & Fat32 Disk: E4 Host: JudgeDee Operator: JRL OS: Windows 2000/NT Date: Sat Jul 21 16:58:28 2001 DISKWIPE.EXE E4_SRC JudgeDee 80 E4 /src /noask /comment Windows 2000 source disk X:\pm\pqmagic /cmd=X:\pm\nt-src.txt Load Operating System to Source disk cmd: X:\ss\DISKHASH.EXE Hash Wimsey 80 /comment E4 /new_log /before Disk hash = 25BF8AF6B2D3E0BD1909C96E368DB27F51C49CBF
Destination Setup:	Z:\ss\DISKWIPE.EXE DI-163 AndWife 81 9F /noask /dst /new_log /comment JRL No partition table defined
Error Setup:	none
Execute:	Z:\ss\DISKWIPE.EXE DI-163 AndWife 81 9F /noask /dst /new_log /comment JRL z:\ss\DISKCMP.EXE DI-163 Cadfael 81 E4 80 9F /new_log /comment JRL
Log files loc:	test-archive/encase/encase-3.20/DI-163
Log File Highlights:	Image file acquired from DOS Restore environment Windows 2000 EnCase report for case DI-163 is in E4.txt Evidence Number "1" Alias "E4 image" File "D:\E4.E01" was acquired by JRL at 05/25/02 04:43:12PM. The computer system clock read: 05/25/02 04:43:12PM. Evidence acquired under DOS 7.10 using version 3.20. File Integrity: Completely Verified, 0 Errors. Verification Hash: AA49F2184A3A4256117B33D906CF7884 Drive Geometry: Total Size 8.6GB (17,938,985 sectors)

Case DI-163 for EnCase 3.20

Partitions:

Code	Type	Start Sector	Total Sectors	Size
0B	FAT32	0	6152895	2.9GB
07	NTFS	10249470	1237005	604.0MB
17	Hidden IFS	13542795	1638630	800.1MB
1B	HiddenFAT32	16691535	1237005	604.0MB

EnCase Report
Case: E4   Page

= = = = Measurement Logs = = = =
Sectors Compared 17938985
Sectors Differ 0
Diffs range
Source (17938985) has 21163351 fewer sectors than destination
(39102336)
Zero fill: 0
Src Byte fill (E4):   0
Dst Byte fill (9F): 21163351
Other fill: 0
Other no fill: 0
This case uses the hash computed from case DI-121
Hash after test: 25BF8AF6B2D3E0BD1909C96E368DB27F51C49CBF

Expected Results:	Source disk is unchanged src compares qualified equal to dst
Actual Results:	No anomalies
Analysis:	Expected results achieved

Case DI-164 for EnCase 3.20

Case Summary:	Create an image from an XBIOS-SCSI source disk to an XBIOS-IDE destination disk where the source disk is larger than the destination
Tester Name:	JRL
Test Date:	Sun Jun 16 19:27:55 2002
PC:	McMillan
Disks:	Source: DOS Drive 80 Physical Label CC Destination: DOS Drive 81 Physical Label 91 Image media: DOS Drive 80 Physical Label 75 CC is a SEAGATE ST336705LC with 71687370 sectors 91 is a WDC WD300BB-00CAA0 with 58633344 sectors 75 is a IC35L040AVER07-0 with 80418240 sectors CD-ROM with PartitionMagic Pro 6.0 and boot floppy with run scripts FS-TST Release 1.0 CD-ROM + Baddisk 3.2 + Badx13 3.2
Source disk setup:	Diskwipe only, no OS Disk: CC Host: McMillan Operator: JRL OS: NoOs Options: none Date: Tue Jun 11 18:07:29 2002 cmd: Z:\ss\DISKWIPE.EXE CC McMillan 80 CC /src /new_log No partitions defined No OS loaded cmd: Z:\ss\DISKHASH.EXE CC McMillan 80 /before /new_log Disk hash = 6001BF9E36538F36751C6FEC94E4CE6DCFC85C9A
Destination Setup:	Z:\ss\DISKWIPE.EXE DI-164 McMillan 81 91 /noask /dst /new_log /comment JRL No partition table defined
Error Setup:	none
Execute:	Z:\ss\DISKWIPE.EXE DI-164 McMillan 81 91 /noask /dst /new_log /comment JRL Z:\ss\DISKCMP.EXE DI-164 HecRamsey 81 CC 80 91 /new_log /comment JRL Z:\ss\DISKHASH.EXE DI-164 HecRamsey 80 /comment CC(JRL) /new log /after
Log files loc:	test-archive/encase/encase-3.20/DI-164
Log File	Image file acquired from DOS

Case DI-164 for EnCase 3.20	
Highlights:	Restore environment Windows 2000 EnCase report for case DI-164 is in CC.txt Evidence Number "CC-drive" Alias "CC-drive" File "F:\CC.E01" was acquired by JRL at 06/15/02 11:39:43PM. The computer system clock read: 06/15/02 11:39:43PM. Evidence acquired under DOS 7.10 using version 3.20. Acquisition Notes: CC has no partition table. File Integrity: Completely Verified, 0 Errors. Verification Hash: 8042F5444887D2B81BB9489D6F844467 Drive Geometry: Total Size 34.2GB (71,687,370 sectors) Unable to read the partition table. EnCase Report Case: CC Page = = = = Measurement Logs = = = = Sectors Compared 58633344 Sectors Differ 12159 Diffs range 58621185-58633343 Source (71687370) has 13054026 more sectors than destination (58633344) Hash computed for this case (DI-164) Hash after test: 6001BF9E36538F36751C6FEC94E4CE6DCFC85C9A
Expected Results:	Source disk is unchanged src compares qualified equal to dst, src is truncated on dst truncation is logged
Actual Results:	Restore anomaly
Analysis:	Expected results not achieved

About the National Institute of Justice

NIJ is the research, development, and evaluation agency of the U.S. Department of Justice. The Institute provides objective, independent, evidence-based knowledge and tools to enhance the administration of justice and public safety. NIJ's principal authorities are derived from the Omnibus Crime Control and Safe Streets Act of 1968, as amended (see 42 U.S.C. §§ 3721–3723).

The NIJ Director is appointed by the President and confirmed by the Senate. The Director establishes the Institute's objectives, guided by the priorities of the Office of Justice Programs, the U.S. Department of Justice, and the needs of the field. The Institute actively solicits the views of criminal justice and other professionals and researchers to inform its search for the knowledge and tools to guide policy and practice.

Strategic Goals

NIJ has seven strategic goals grouped into three categories:

Creating relevant knowledge and tools

1. Partner with State and local practitioners and policymakers to identify social science research and technology needs.
2. Create scientific, relevant, and reliable knowledge—with a particular emphasis on terrorism, violent crime, drugs and crime, cost-effectiveness, and community-based efforts—to enhance the administration of justice and public safety.
3. Develop affordable and effective tools and technologies to enhance the administration of justice and public safety.

Dissemination

4. Disseminate relevant knowledge and information to practitioners and policymakers in an understandable, timely, and concise manner.
5. Act as an honest broker to identify the information, tools, and technologies that respond to the needs of stakeholders.

Agency management

6. Practice fairness and openness in the research and development process.
7. Ensure professionalism, excellence, accountability, cost-effectiveness, and integrity in the management and conduct of NIJ activities and programs.

Program Areas

In addressing these strategic challenges, the Institute is involved in the following program areas: crime control and prevention, including policing; drugs and crime; justice systems and offender behavior, including corrections; violence and victimization; communications and information technologies; critical incident response; investigative and forensic sciences, including DNA; less-than-lethal technologies; officer protection; education and training technologies; testing and standards; technology assistance to law enforcement and corrections agencies; field testing of promising programs; and international crime control.

In addition to sponsoring research and development and technology assistance, NIJ evaluates programs, policies, and technologies. NIJ communicates its research and evaluation findings through conferences and print and electronic media.

To find out more about the National Institute of Justice, please contact:

National Criminal Justice
  Reference Service
P.O. Box 6000
Rockville, MD 20849–6000
800–851–3420
e-mail: *askncjrs@ncjrs.org*